Sophie's
Sweet and
Savory Loaves

Sophie's Sweet and Savory Loaves

SOPHIE DUDEMAINE

PHOTOGRAPHS BY
CHRISTOPHE MADAMOUR

TRANSLATION BY
LINDA DANNENBERG AND
JOANNA PRUESS

Éditions Minerva · Geneva, Switzerland

Table of Contents

Summer

5

Autumn

Winter

Preface

What could be simpler, more eloquent and comforting in its unpretentious appeal, than a pound cake? It's an ideal and versatile confection, perfect for a light snack or teatime indulgence, or, in the case of the savory "loaves" presented in this book, an integral part of a good lunch or fine supper. When guided by the hand and imagination of Sophie Dudemaine, the traditionally sweet pound cake is easily adapted to a savory mode.

In Auch, when Sophie was part of my kitchen brigade at the Hôtel de France, I oversaw the work of this beautiful baking artist. Later, on her own, she intuitively discovered and perfected the art of the pound cake. Sophie had mastered the techniques of baking, and knew how to harmonize flavors. It remained only for her to invent her recipes, and her creativity today seems boundless. Seventy-six of her favorites are featured in this book, which should serve both as a cookbook and as a source of inspiration for your own creations.

I urge you to hurry to your ovens, find your loaf pans and decorative cake molds, and begin discovering some of Sophie's delicious savory loaves and sweet cakes. To me they represent the perfect union of great taste and conviviality—two qualities without which life would indeed be very dull!

André Daguin

Spring

Salmon and Sorrel Loaf

Serves 6 to 8

2 tablespoons salted butter

1/2 pound sorrel

1/2 pound salmon fillet, skin removed,
cut into bite-size pieces

Fine sea salt

Freshly ground black pepper

3 large eggs

1 cup plus 2 tablespoons all-purpose flour, sifted

2 teaspoons baking powder

1/3 cup plus 2 tablespoons
sunflower oil

1/2 cup milk, hot

1 1/4 cups shredded Gruyère cheese

1. Preheat the oven to 350°F. In a large nonaluminum skillet, melt the butter over medium heat. Add the sorrel, stir to coat, and cook for 3 to 4 minutes, until the leaves wilt. Add the salmon, stir gently to combine, and cook for about 5 minutes, until the salmon has just cooked through. Season with 2 pinches each of salt and pepper and set aside.

2. In the bowl of an electric mixer, combine the eggs, flour, and baking powder and beat until well blended. Gradually add the oil, beating constantly to blend. Gradually add the milk, beating constantly to blend, then add the cheese and stir with a wooden spoon to incorporate.

3. Scrape the batter into an ungreased 8 1/2-by-4 1/2-inch loaf pan. Bake in the center of the oven for 45 to 55 minutes, until a toothpick inserted into the center comes out clean. Transfer the pan to a wire rack and let cool for at least 15 minutes, then slide a thin knife around the loaf and remove from the pan. Serve warm or at room temperature.

*Variations: For a Salmon-Tarragon Loaf, omit the sorrel and
add 1/2 cup chopped fresh tarragon. For a Salmon-Leek Loaf, omit the sorrel
and add the chopped white and pale green portions of 2 leeks,
sautéed in butter for 4 minutes.*

Sea Scallop, Leek, and Parmesan Loaf

Serves 6 to 8

1 tablespoon extra-virgin
olive oil

1/2 pound sea scallops,
diced large

1/2 teaspoon curry powder

2 tablespoons salted butter

2 medium leeks, white and
pale green parts only, well washed,
dried, thinly sliced

Fine sea salt

Freshly ground black pepper

3 large eggs

1 cup plus 2 tablespoons
all-purpose flour, sifted

2 teaspoons baking powder

1/3 cup plus 2 tablespoons
sunflower oil

1/2 cup milk, hot

1 1/4 cups shredded
Gruyère cheese

1/2 cup grated Parmesan cheese

1. Preheat the oven to 350°F. In a large skillet, heat the olive oil over medium-high heat. Add the scallops and sauté, stirring frequently, for 1 minute. Add the curry powder, stir to combine, then transfer the mixture to a bowl and set aside.

2. In the same skillet used for the scallops, melt the butter over medium heat. Add the leeks and stir to coat. Add 1/3 cup plus 2 tablespoons water and cook, stirring occasionally, for 10 minutes. Season with 2 pinches each of salt and pepper. Add the leeks to the reserved scallops, stir to combine, and set aside.

3. In the bowl of an electric mixer, combine the eggs, flour, and baking powder and beat until well blended. Gradually add the oil, beating constantly to blend. Gradually add the milk, beating constantly to blend, then add the cheeses and stir with a wooden spoon to incorporate. Add the scallop mixture to the batter and stir gently with a wooden spoon to combine.

4. Scrape the batter into an ungreased 8 1/2-by-4 1/2-inch loaf pan. Bake in the center of the oven for 45 to 55 minutes, until a toothpick inserted into the center comes out clean. Transfer the pan to a wire rack and let cool for 15 minutes, then slide a thin knife around the loaf and remove from the pan. Serve warm or at room temperature.

Chicken and Tarragon Loaf

Serves 6 to 8

1 tablespoon salted butter	1/3 cup tarragon, chopped
1/3 cup plus 3 tablespoons sunflower oil	3 large eggs
1 shallot, minced	1 cup plus 2 tablespoons all-purpose flour, sifted
1/2 pound boneless chicken breast, sliced into 1/4-inch strips	2 teaspoons baking powder
Fine sea salt	1/2 cup milk, hot
Freshly ground black pepper	1 1/4 cups shredded Gruyère cheese

1. Preheat the oven to 350°F. In a large skillet, combine the butter and 1 tablespoon oil and heat over medium heat. Add the shallot and sauté, stirring frequently, until the shallot is soft and slightly translucent, about 4 to 5 minutes. Add the chicken, season with 2 pinches each of salt and pepper, then sauté, stirring frequently, for 5 minutes. Add the tarragon, stir to combine, then remove from the heat and set aside.

2. In the bowl of an electric mixer, combine the eggs, flour, and baking powder and beat until well blended. Gradually add the remaining 1/3 cup plus 2 tablespoons oil, beating constantly to blend. Gradually add the milk, beating constantly to blend, then add the cheese and stir with a wooden spoon to incorporate. Add the chicken mixture and stir gently with a wooden spoon to combine.

3. Pour the batter into an ungreased 8 1/2-by-4 1/2-inch loaf pan. Bake in the center of the oven for 45 to 55 minutes, until a toothpick inserted into the center comes out clean. Transfer the pan to a wire rack and let cool for at least 15 minutes, then slide a thin knife around the loaf and remove from the pan. Serve warm or at room temperature.

Bacon and Prune Loaf

Serves 6 to 8

3 large eggs

1 cup plus 2 tablespoons all-purpose flour, sifted

2 teaspoons baking powder

Fine sea salt

Freshly ground black pepper

1/3 cup plus 3 tablespoons sunflower oil

1/2 cup milk, hot

1 1/4 cups shredded Gruyère cheese

1/3 pound slab bacon, rind removed,
cut into 1-by-1/4-by-1/4-inch strips

3 ounces prunes, diced large

1. Preheat the oven to 350°F. In the bowl of an electric mixer, combine the eggs, flour, baking powder and a pinch of salt and two pinches of pepper. Gradually add the oil, beating constantly to blend. Gradually add the milk, beating constantly to blend, then add the cheese and stir with a wooden spoon to incorporate. Set aside.

2. Heat a medium skillet over medium heat, add the bacon, and sauté, stirring frequently, for about 5 minutes, until the bacon is lightly browned. Add the prunes and stir to combine. Remove from the heat, then add the mixture to the reserved batter and stir gently with a wooden spoon to combine.

3. Scrape the batter into an ungreased 8 1/2-by-4 1/2-inch loaf pan. Bake in the center of the oven for 45 to 55 minutes, until a toothpick inserted into the center comes out clean. Transfer the pan to a wire rack and let cool for at least 15 minutes, then slide a thin knife around the loaf and remove from the pan. Serve warm or at room temperature.

Variation: For a Bacon, Prune, and Hazelnut Loaf,
add 1/3 cup chopped hazelnuts to the batter, and reduce the
amount of prunes by one-third, to 2 ounces.

SOPHIES SWEET AND
SAVORY LOAVES

Orange Pound Cake

Serves 6 to 8

3 large eggs

3/4 cup plus 1 tablespoon sugar

1 1/4 cups all-purpose flour, sifted

3/4 teaspoon baking powder

1 stick plus 3 tablespoons (11 tablespoons) salted butter, melted

Finely grated zest of 1 orange

Juice of 1 orange

1. Preheat the oven to 350°F. In the bowl of an electric mixer, combine the eggs and sugar and beat until the mixture is creamy and pale yellow. Sprinkle in the flour and the baking powder, beating constantly to blend. Add the butter and beat to blend, then add the orange zest and the orange juice and beat to blend.

2. Scrape the batter into a buttered and floured 8 1/2-by-4 1/2-inch loaf pan. Bake 40 to 50 minutes, until a toothpick inserted into the center comes out clean. Transfer the pan to a wire rack and let cool for 15 minutes, then slide a thin knife around the cake, invert, and remove from the pan; return the cake, right side up, to the wire rack to cool completely. Serve at room temperature.

*Variations: For an Orange-Honey-Walnut Cake,
add 1 tablespoon honey and 1/3 cup chopped walnuts to the batter
with the orange zest. For an Orange-Cinnamon-Raisin-Date Cake, add a pinch
of ground cinnamon, 1/4 cup raisins (plumped for 1/2 hour in warm water,
then drained), and 1/4 cup chopped pitted dates to the batter with
the orange zest. For an Orange-Chocolate Chip Cake, add
1/3 cup chocolate chips to the batter
with the orange zest.*

Banana Pound Cake

Serves 4 to 6

2 tablespoons salted butter, chilled

2 medium bananas, cut into 1/4-inch slices

3/4 cup plus 1 tablespoon sugar

3 large eggs

1 1/4 cups all-purpose flour, sifted

2/3 teaspoon baking powder

1 stick plus 4 tablespoons (12 tablespoons)
salted butter, melted

1. Preheat the oven to 350°F. In a medium skillet, melt the chilled butter over medium heat. Sprinkle the bananas with 1 tablespoon of the sugar, add to the skillet, and stir to coat with the butter. Sauté, stirring frequently, for about 5 minutes, until the bananas are softened and slightly caramelized. Set aside to cool.

2. In the bowl of an electric mixer, combine the eggs and the remaining 3/4 cup sugar and beat until the mixture is creamy and pale yellow. Gradually add the flour and the baking powder, beating constantly to blend. Add the melted butter, beating to blend. Add the caramelized bananas and stir gently with a wooden spoon to incorporate.

3. Scrape into a buttered and floured 8 1/2-by-4 1/2-inch loaf pan, or into 4 to 6 smaller figurative molds, such as a bunny or a cat mold. Bake in the center of the oven for 40 to 55 minutes (less cooking time for smaller molds), until a toothpick inserted into the center comes out clean. Transfer the pan to a wire rack and let cool for 15 minutes, then slide a thin knife around the cake, invert, and remove the cake; return the cake, right side up, to the wire rack to cool completely. Serve at room temperature.

Variations: : For a Banana Chocolate Pound Cake,
melt a 3 1/2-ounce bar of dark chocolate and stir into the batter
just before you add the bananas.

21

SOPHIES SWEET AND
SAVORY LOAVES

Vanilla Pound Cake

Serves 6 to 8

3 large eggs

3/4 cup plus 1 tablespoon sugar

1 1/4 cups all-purpose flour, sifted

3/4 teaspoon baking powder

1 1/2 sticks (12 tablespoons) salted butter, melted

1 vanilla bean, split lengthwise, seeds scraped out and reserved;
pod reserved for another use; or 1 teaspoon vanilla extract

1. Preheat the oven to 350°F. In the bowl of an electric mixer, combine the eggs and sugar and beat until the mixture is creamy and pale yellow. Gradually add the flour and the baking powder, beating constantly to blend. Add the melted butter and beat to blend, then add the vanilla seeds and beat to blend.

2. Scrape the mixture into a buttered and floured 8 1/2-by-4 1/2-inch loaf pan. Bake in the center of the oven for 40 to 55 minutes, until a toothpick inserted into the center comes out clean. Transfer the pan to a wire rack and let cool for 15 minutes. Slide a thin knife around the cake, invert, and remove the cake; return the cake, right side up, to the wire rack to cool completely. Serve at room temperature.

Variation: : *You can produce a basic
Classic Pound Cake by simply omitting the vanilla.*

SOPHIES SWEET AND
SAVORY LOAVES

Spinach, Watercress, and Fennel Loaf

Serves 6 to 8

Fine sea salt

1 bunch watercress, stems trimmed

1 pound spinach

4 tablespoons salted butter

Freshly ground black pepper

Freshly grated nutmeg

1 medium fennel bulb,
trimmed, diced large

1 teaspoon sesame seeds

3 large eggs

1 cup plus 2 tablespoons
all-purpose flour, sifted

1 3/4 teaspoons baking powder

1/3 cup sunflower oil

1/2 cup milk, hot

1 1/4 cups grated Gruyère cheese

1. Bring a casserole of salted water to a boil over high heat, add the watercress and the spinach, and blanch for 1 minute. Drain, then dry well with paper towels. In a large skillet, melt 2 tablespoons of the butter, add the spinach and watercress, and stir to coat. Add 2 pinches each of salt and pepper, and 1 pinch of nutmeg and stir to combine. Cook, stirring frequently, for 4 minutes. Transfer to a bowl and set aside.

2. Bring a saucepan of salted water to a boil over high heat. Add the fennel and cook for 5 minutes. Drain, refresh with cold water, and dry well with paper towels. In the skillet used for the spinach mixture, melt the remaining 2 tablespoons butter, add the fennel, stir to coat, then add 2 pinches each of salt and pepper, and the sesame seeds, and stir to combine. Reduce the heat to low and cook, stirring frequently, for 15 minutes, then drain.

3. Preheat the oven to 350°F. In the bowl of an electric mixer, combine the eggs, flour, and baking powder and beat until well blended. Gradually add the oil, beating constantly to blend. Gradually add the milk, beating constantly to blend, then add the cheese and stir with a wooden spoon to incorporate. Add the spinach mixture and the fennel and stir gently to combine.

4. Scrape the batter into an ungreased 8 1/2-by-4 1/2-inch loaf pan. Bake in the center of the oven for 45 to 55 minutes, until a toothpick inserted into the center comes out clean. Transfer the pan to a wire rack and let cool for at least 15 minutes, then slide a thin knife around the loaf and remove from the pan. Serve warm or at room temperature.

Crabmeat and Chive Loaf

Serves 6 to 8

3 large eggs

1 cup plus 2 tablespoons all-purpose flour, sifted

2 teaspoons baking powder

Fine sea salt

Freshly ground black pepper

1/3 cup plus 2 tablespoons sunflower oil

1/2 cup milk, hot

1 1/4 cups shredded Gruyère cheese

1/2 pound freshly cooked, or canned, crabmeat, drained

2 tablespoons finely chopped chives

1. Preheat the oven to 350°F. In the bowl of an electric mixer, combine the eggs, flour, baking powder, and 2 pinches each of salt and pepper and beat until well blended. Gradually add the oil, beating constantly to blend, then gradually add the milk, beating constantly to blend. Add the cheese and stir gently with a wooden spoon to combine. Add the crabmeat and the chives, and stir gently to incorporate.

2. Scrape the batter into an ungreased 8 1/2-by-4 1/2-inch loaf pan. Bake in the center of the oven for 45 to 55 minutes, until a toothpick inserted into the center comes out clean. Transfer the pan to a wire rack and let cool for 15 minutes, then slide a thin knife around the loaf and remove from the pan. Serve warm or at room temperature.

SOPHIES SWEET AND
SAVORY LOAVES

Artichoke and Olive Loaf

Serves 6 to 8

Fine sea salt

Juice of 1 lemon

1/2 pound frozen baby artichokes

3 large eggs

1 cup plus 2 tablespoons
all-purpose flour, sifted

1 3/4 teaspoons baking powder

Freshly ground black pepper

1/3 cup plus 2 tablespoons
sunflower oil

1/2 cup milk, hot

1 1/4 cups shredded Gruyère cheese

12 pimento-stuffed green olives,
coarsely chopped

1. To a saucepan of boiling salted water, add the lemon juice and the artichokes and cook just until crisp-tender, about 5 minutes. Drain well, pat dry with paper towels, reserve 2 artichokes, then chop the remaining artichokes coarsely. In a food processor, puree the chopped artichokes and set aside.

2. Preheat the oven to 350°F. In the bowl of an electric mixer, combine the eggs, flour, baking powder, and 2 pinches each of salt and pepper and beat until well blended. Gradually add the oil, beating constantly to blend, then add the milk, beating constantly to blend. Add the cheese and stir with a wooden spoon to incorporate. Add the artichoke puree and stir to combine.

3. Scrape half of the batter into an ungreased 8 1/2-by-4 1/2-inch loaf pan. Thinly slice the 2 reserved artichokes and scatter over the batter, then scatter on the olives. Scrape in the remaining batter. Bake in the center of the oven for 45 to 55 minutes, until a toothpick inserted into the center comes out clean. Transfer the pan to a wire rack and let cool for at least 15 minutes, then slide a thin knife around the loaf and remove from the pan. Serve warm or at room temperature.

Sweet Potato Cake

Serves 6 to 8

3/4 cup raisins	6 tablespoons all-purpose flour, sifted
1/4 cup dark rum	1/3 cup plus 2 tablespoons milk
Fine sea salt	2 large eggs
5 small sweet potatoes or yams, scrubbed	2 large egg yolks
1/2 teaspoon paprika	2 large egg whites
1 tablespoon sugar	1 tablespoon salted butter for the pan

1. In a small mixing bowl, combine the raisins, rum, and 1/2 cup hot water and set aside for 30 minutes to soften and plump the raisins.

2. In a large pot of boiling salted water, cook the sweet potatoes, covered, for about 20 minutes, until they are tender when pierced with a thin skewer. Drain, peel, quarter, and place in a large mixing bowl. Finely mash the potatoes with a potato ricer, food mill, or potato masher, removing all lumps. Add the paprika, sugar, flour, and milk and whisk to combine. One at a time, whisk in the 2 eggs, followed by the 2 egg yolks, then set aside.

3. Preheat the oven to 400°F. Fill a deep-sided baking pan with 1 1/2 inches of boiling water and place in the center of the oven. In the bowl of an electric mixer, beat the egg whites until they hold firm but not stiff peaks. Add half of the egg whites to the sweet potato mixture and gently fold in, then fold in the remaining egg whites, working carefully to maintain as much volume as possible. Drain the raisins, add to the batter, and gently fold in.

4. Scrape the batter into a buttered 8 1/2-by-4 1/2-inch loaf pan. Place the loaf pan in the center of the water-filled baking pan and bake for 40 to 50 minutes, until a toothpick inserted into the center comes out clean. Transfer the pan to a wire rack and let cool for at least 15 minutes, then slide a thin knife around the cake, invert, and remove from the pan; return the cake, right side up, to the wire rack to cool completely. Serve at room temperature.

Caramelized Rice Cake

Serves 6 to 8

1 cup Arborio rice, rinsed well

3 cups milk

3/4 cup sugar

1 vanilla bean, split lengthwise

3 large egg yolks

1 tablespoon crème fraîche
or heavy cream

3 large egg whites

1 tablespoon salted butter for the pan

For the caramel sauce:

1/2 cup sugar

Juice of 1/2 lemon

1. Bring a medium saucepan of water to a boil, add the rice, cook for 5 minutes, then drain and set aside. In a large saucepan, combine the milk, sugar, and the vanilla bean and bring to a boil over medium-high heat. Add the rice, stir to combine, cover, reduce the heat to low, and cook without stirring for 30 minutes. Remove from the heat, remove and discard the vanilla bean, then add the egg yolks and the crème fraîche and stir well to incorporate. Set aside to cool.

2. In the bowl of an electric mixer, beat the egg whites until they hold firm but not stiff peaks. Add half of the egg whites to the cooled rice mixture and gently fold in. Add the remaining egg whites to the rice mixture and gently fold in, working carefully to maintain as much volume as possible. Set aside.

3. Preheat the oven to 400°F. Fill a deep-sided baking pan with 1 1/2 inches of boiling water and place in the center of the oven. Butter an 8 1/2-by-4 1/2-inch loaf pan, or a 6-cup tube pan or fluted mold, and set aside.

To make the caramel sauce:

1. In a small saucepan, combine the sugar, lemon juice, and 1/4 cup water. Bring to a boil over medium-high heat, then reduce the heat to medium-low and cook without stirring until the mixture thickens and caramelizes to a golden brown. Using a teaspoon, immediately drizzle the caramel over the bottom and sides of the loaf pan. (You must work quickly, since the caramel hardens in a few seconds.)

2. Scrape in the batter, place the loaf pan in the center of the water-filled baking pan, and bake for 45 to 55 minutes, until a toothpick inserted into the center comes out clean. Transfer to a wire rack to cool. To unmold, place the loaf pan for 1 minute into a baking pan filled with boiling water. Invert the pan and ease the cake out, upside down, onto a serving plate. Drizzle any caramel left in the pan over the cake and serve.

Butterless Pound Cake

Serves 6 to 8

4 large egg yolks

1 1/4 cups granulated sugar

1/2 cup all-purpose flour, sifted

1/2 cup potato flour, sifted

3/4 teaspoon baking powder

4 large egg whites

2 tablespoons vanilla sugar,
or granulated light brown sugar

*Note: If you substitute granulated brown sugar for the vanilla sugar,
add 1/2 teaspoon vanilla extract to the batter.*

1. Preheat the oven to 325°F. Butter and flour an 8 1/2-by-4 1/2-inch loaf pan and set aside. In the bowl of an electric mixer, combine the egg yolks and the granulated sugar and beat until creamy and pale yellow. Add the all-purpose flour, potato flour, and baking powder and beat to blend. Add the vanilla, if using. Set the batter aside.

2. In the bowl of an electric mixer, beat the egg whites until they hold firm but not stiff peaks. Add 1 cup of the egg whites to the batter and gently fold in. Add the remaining egg whites to the batter and gently fold in, working carefully to maintain as much volume as possible. Sprinkle the vanilla sugar over the bottom and the sides of the loaf pan.

3. Scrape the batter into the pan. Bake in the center of the oven for about 1 hour, until a toothpick inserted into the center comes out clean. Transfer the pan to a wire rack and let cool for at least 15 minutes, then slide a thin knife around the loaf, invert, and remove from the pan; return the cake, right side up, to the wire rack to cool completely. Serve at room temperature.

35

SOPHIE'S SWEET AND
SAVORY LOAVES

Warm Chocolate Pound Cake

Serves 6 to 8

1 tablespoon salted butter for the pan

2 large eggs

3/4 cup plus 2 tablespoons sugar

1 (6-ounce) container plain yogurt (3/4 cup)

1 cup plus 2 tablespoons all-purpose flour, sifted

3/4 teaspoon baking powder

1/3 cup plus 2 tablespoons sunflower oil

1 (7-ounce) bar dark chocolate, chopped, then melted

1. Preheat the oven to 350°F. Butter and flour an 8 1/2-by-4 1/2-inch loaf pan and set aside. In the bowl of an electric mixer, combine the eggs and the sugar and beat until the mixture is creamy and pale yellow. Add the yogurt and beat to blend, then add the flour and baking powder and beat to blend. Gradually add the oil, beating until the batter is very smooth, with no lumps. Gradually pour in the melted chocolate, stirring constantly to incorporate.

2. Scrape into the loaf pan. Bake in the center of the oven for 35 to 45 minutes, until a toothpick inserted into the center comes out clean. Transfer the pan to a wire rack and let cool for 15 minutes, then slide a thin knife around the loaf, invert, and remove from the pan; return the cake, right side up, to the wire rack to cool to lukewarm. Serve lukewarm, while the center of the cake is still warm and unctuous, almost like a pudding-cake.

*Variation: : For White Chocolate and Hazelnut Cake,
omit the dark chocolate and add 5 ounces melted white chocolate and
3 ounces whole hazelnuts. For Chocolate and Candied Orange Peel Cake, before baking
sprinkle the top of the batter in the loaf pan with 1/2 cup diced candied orange peel.
For Chocolate Pear Cake, add 2 peeled, cored, and diced ripe Anjou or
Bartlett pears to the batter before baking.*

Tuna and Bell Pepper Loaf

Serves 6 to 8

1/2 small green bell pepper	3 large eggs
1 pound red bell peppers (about 3 small peppers)	1 cup plus 2 tablespoons all-purpose flour, sifted
2 tablespoons extra-virgin olive oil	1 3/4 teaspoons baking powder
1/2 pound fresh tuna, cut into bite-size pieces	1/3 cup plus 2 tablespoons sunflower oil
Fine sea salt	1/2 cup milk, hot
Freshly ground black pepper	1 1/4 cups grated Gruyère cheese

1. Preheat the broiler. Place the green and red peppers directly on the oven rack under the broiler and cook, turning occasionally, until the skins turn brown and blistered. Cool until the peppers can be handled, then peel, core, seed, and cut into very thin slices. In a skillet, heat the olive oil over medium heat, then add the peppers, stir to coat, and sauté, stirring frequently, for 20 minutes. Meanwhile, toward the end of the cooking time, preheat the oven to 350°F. Add the tuna, two pinches each of salt and pepper, stir to combine, and cook, stirring occasionally, for 5 minutes. Set aside.

2. In the bowl of an electric mixer, combine the eggs, flour, and baking powder, and beat to blend. Gradually add the sunflower oil, beating to blend, then add the milk, beating to blend. Add the cheese and stir to combine, then add the tuna mixture and stir in carefully to evenly incorporate.

3. Scrape the batter into an ungreased 8 1/2-by-4 1/2-inch loaf pan. Bake in the center of the oven for 45 to 55 minutes, until a toothpick inserted into the center comes out clean. Transfer the pan to a wire rack and let cool for about 15 minutes, then slide a thin knife around the loaf, invert, and remove from the pan. Serve warm or at room temperature.

Variations: For Tuna and Tomato Loaf, omit the peppers and add 2 large tomatoes, peeled, seeded, coarsely chopped, and sautéed for 15 minutes in a little olive oil; and 6 finely julienned basil leaves. For Tuna and Chive Loaf, omit the peppers and add 1/3 cup chopped chives.

SOPHIE'S SWEET AND SAVORY LOAVES

Tomato, Anchovy, and Black Olive Loaf

Serves 6 to 8

1/3 cup plus 3 tablespoons sunflower oil

2 large ripe tomatoes, peeled
(plunge into boiling water for 30 seconds to facilitate peeling),
seeded, and diced

2 (2-ounce) tins anchovy fillets, drained and chopped

1/3 cup oil-cured black olives, pitted and halved

Freshly ground black pepper

3 large eggs

1 cup plus 2 tablespoons all-purpose flour, sifted

1 3/4 teaspoons baking powder

1/2 cup milk, hot

1 1/4 cups grated Gruyère cheese

1. In a skillet, heat 1 tablespoon of the oil over medium heat. Add the tomatoes, stir to coat, then cook, stirring frequently, for 15 minutes. Add the anchovies, olives, and several pinches of pepper, stir to combine, then remove from the heat and set aside.

2. Preheat the oven to 350°F. In the bowl of an electric mixer, combine the eggs, flour, and baking powder and beat to blend. Gradually add the remaining 1/3 cup plus 2 tablespoons oil, beating constantly, and then add the milk, beating until smooth. Add the cheese and stir to combine. Add the tomato mixture and gently stir to evenly incorporate.

3. Scrape the mixture into an ungreased 8 1/2-by-4 1/2-inch loaf pan. Bake in the center of the oven for 45 to 55 minutes until a toothpick inserted into the center comes out clean. Transfer the pan to a wire rack and let cool for at least 15 minutes, then slide a thin knife around the loaf, invert, and remove from the pan. Serve warm or at room temperature.

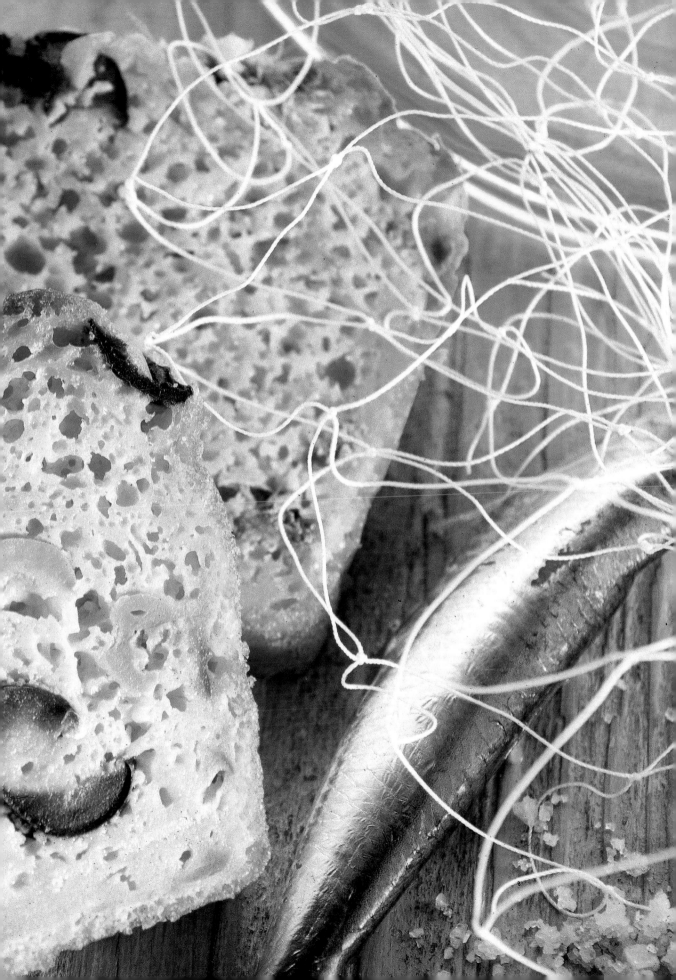

Black Cherry and Ginger Cake

Serves 6 to 8

3 large eggs

3/4 cup plus 2 tablespoons sugar

1 cup plus 3 tablespoons all-purpose flour, sifted

1 3/4 teaspoons baking powder

1 stick plus 2 tablespoons (10 tablespoons) salted butter, melted

1 tablespoon freshly grated ginger

1 tablespoon Kirsch

1 cup black cherries, halved, stones removed

1. Preheat the oven to 350°F. Butter and flour a 6-cup heart-shaped cake pan or an 8 1/2-by-4 1/2-inch loaf pan and set aside.

2. In the bowl of an electric mixer, combine the eggs and sugar and beat until creamy and pale yellow. Gradually sprinkle in all but 1 tablespoon of the flour, and the baking powder, beating constantly to blend. Add the melted butter in a thin stream, beating constantly to blend. Stir in the ginger and Kirsch. In a small bowl, toss the cherries with the remaining 1 tablespoon flour to coat, then add them to the batter and gently stir to evenly incorporate.

3. Scrape the batter into the pan. Bake in the center of the oven for 40 to 50 minutes, until a toothpick inserted into the center comes out clean. Transfer the pan to a wire rack and let cool for about 15 minutes, then slide a thin knife around the cake, invert, and remove from the pan; return the cake, right side up, to the wire rack to cool completely. Serve at room temperature

SOPHIE'S SWEET AND
SAVORY LOAVES

Coconut-Chocolate Chip Pound Cake

Serves 6 to 8

1 tablespoon salted butter for the pan

2 large eggs

3/4 cup plus 3 tablespoons sugar

1 (6-ounce) container plain yogurt (3/4 cup)

1 cup plus 2 tablespoons all-purpose flour, sifted

3/4 teaspoon baking powder

1/3 cup plus 2 tablespoons sunflower oil

3/4 cup shredded unsweetened coconut

1/4 cup semisweet chocolate chips

1. Preheat the oven to 350°F. Butter and flour an 8 1/2-by-4 1/2-inch loaf pan and set aside.

2. In the bowl of an electric mixer, combine the eggs and sugar and beat until the mixture is creamy and pale yellow. Add the yogurt, beat to blend, then add the flour and baking powder and beat well to blend. Gradually add the oil, beating until all lumps in the batter are gone. Add the coconut and the chocolate chips, and stir gently to evenly incorporate.

3. Scrape the batter into the pan. Bake in the center of the oven for 45 to 55 minutes, until a toothpick inserted into the center comes out clean. Transfer the pan to a wire rack and let cool for about 15 minutes, then slide a thin knife around the cake, invert, and remove from the pan; return the cake, right side up, to the wire rack to cool completely. Serve at room temperature.

*Variation: For Chocolate Chip Pound Cake, omit the coconut
and increase the amount of chocolate chips to 2/3 cup.
For Coconut Pound Cake, omit the chocolate chips.*

43

SOPHIE'S SWEET AND
SAVORY LOAVES

Almond and Orange-Flower Pound Cake

Serves 6 to 8

6 tablespoons almond paste, cut into small bits

3 large eggs

3/4 cup plus 1 tablespoon confectioners' sugar

1 cup all-purpose flour, sifted

3/4 teaspoon baking powder

1 teaspoon orange-flower water, or 1 teaspoon orange extract

Zest and juice of 1 lemon

7 tablespoons unsalted butter, melted

1/2 cup sliced almonds

1. Preheat the oven to 350°F. In the bowl of an electric mixer, place the almond paste and begin beating at low speed to soften. One at a time, add the eggs, beating constantly to combine, then continue beating, scraping down the sides of the bowl occasionally, for 5 minutes. Add the sugar, beat to blend, then add the flour, baking powder, orange-flower water, lemon zest, and lemon juice and beat to incorporate. Gradually add the melted butter, beating constantly to blend.

2. Scrape the batter into an ungreased 8 1/2-by-4 1/2-inch loaf pan, then garnish with the sliced almonds. Bake in the center of the oven for 40 to 50 minutes, until a toothpick inserted into the center comes out clean. Transfer the pan to a wire rack and let cool for about 15 minutes, then slide a thin knife around the cake, invert, and remove from the pan; return the cake to the wire rack to cool completely. Serve at room temperature.

Rose Petal Pound Cake

Serves 6 to 8

5 ounces dried rose buds
(unsprayed and untreated with preservatives), petals detached and reserved

3/4 cup plus 2 tablespoons granulated sugar

1 stick plus 1 tablespoon (9 tablespoons) salted butter, softened

1 cup confectioners' sugar

3 large eggs

1 cup plus 3 tablespoons all-purpose flour, sifted

1 3/4 teaspoons baking powder

Fresh rose buds or petals for garnish (optional)

1. Bring a pot of water to a boil, add the rose petals, and cook for 30 seconds. Drain, pat dry with paper towels, and set aside. In a medium saucepan, combine 1 1/2 cups water with the granulated sugar and bring to a boil over medium heat, stirring to dissolve. Add the rose petals, stir to combine, reduce the heat to low, and simmer for 30 minutes. Set aside to cool.

2. Preheat the oven to 350°F. In the bowl of an electric mixer, cream the butter and the confectioners' sugar. One at a time, add the eggs, beating after each to incorporate. Add the flour and baking powder and beat to combine. Add the rose petal mixture and stir gently to evenly incorporate.

3. Scrape the batter into an ungreased 8 1/2-by-4 1/2-inch loaf pan. Bake in the center of the oven for 45 to 55 minutes, until a toothpick inserted at the center comes out clean. Transfer the pan to a wire rack, and let cool for about 15 minutes, then slide a thin knife around the cake, invert, and remove from the pan; return the cake, right side up, to the wire rack to cool completely. Serve on a platter garnished with rose buds or petals if you wish, at room temperature.

Summer

Rabbit, Prune, and Watercress Loaf

Serves 6 to 8

1 tablespoon extra-virgin olive oil

1/2 pound fresh boned saddle of rabbit, cut into small bits

1 cup watercress leaves and tiny sprigs, coarsely chopped

2/3 cup prunes, pitted and very thinly sliced

Fine sea salt

Freshly ground black pepper

1/2 teaspoon savory

3 large eggs

1 cup plus 2 tablespoons all-purpose flour, sifted

1 3/4 teaspoons baking powder

1/3 cup plus 2 tablespoons sunflower oil

1/2 cup milk, hot

1 1/4 cups grated Gruyère cheese

1. Preheat the oven to 350°F. In a skillet, heat the olive oil over medium-high heat. Add the rabbit, stir to coat, then sauté for about 5 minutes, until the meat is just cooked through and lightly browned. Remove from the heat, add the watercress, prunes, 2 pinches each of salt and pepper, and the savory and stir to combine. Set aside.

2. In the bowl of an electric mixer, combine the eggs, flour, and baking powder and beat to blend. Gradually add the sunflower oil, beating to blend, then add the milk, beating to blend. Add the cheese and stir to combine, then add the rabbit mixture and stir gently to evenly incorporate.

3. Scrape the mixture into an ungreased 8 1/2-by-4 1/2-inch loaf pan. Bake in the center of the oven for 45 to 55 minutes, until a toothpick inserted into the center comes out clean. Transfer the pan to a wire rack and let cool for about 15 minutes, then slide a thin knife around the loaf, invert, and remove from the pan. Serve warm or at room temperature.

Ham and Olive Loaf

Serves 6 to 8

3 large eggs

1 cup plus 2 tablespoons all-purpose flour, sifted

1 3/4 teaspoons baking powder

Fine sea salt

Freshly ground black pepper

1/3 cup plus 2 tablespoons sunflower oil

1/2 cup milk, hot

1 1/4 cups grated Gruyère cheese

1/3 pound baked ham, diced small

3/4 cup green olives, pitted and chopped

1. Preheat the oven to 350°F. In the bowl of an electric mixer, combine the eggs, flour, baking powder, and 2 pinches each of salt and pepper and beat to blend. Gradually add the oil, beating to blend, then add the milk, beating to blend. Add the cheese and stir to combine. Add the ham and the olives and stir to evenly incorporate.

2. Scrape the batter into an ungreased 8 1/2-by-4 1/2-inch loaf pan. Bake in the center of the oven for 45 to 55 minutes, until a toothpick inserted into the center comes out clean. Transfer the pan to a wire rack and let cool for about 15 minutes, then slide a thin knife around the loaf, invert, and remove from the pan. Serve warm or at room temperature.

***Variation:** For Ham, Edam Cheese, and Pistachio Loaf,
omit the olives and add 1/2 cup coarsely chopped Edam cheese and
1/2 cup coarsely chopped pistachio nuts to the batter. For Bacon and Olive Loaf,
omit the ham and add 1/3 pound slab bacon, rind removed,
diced small, and sautéed for 5 minutes over medium
heat until browned, to the batter.*

53

SOPHIE'S SWEET AND
SAVORY LOAVES

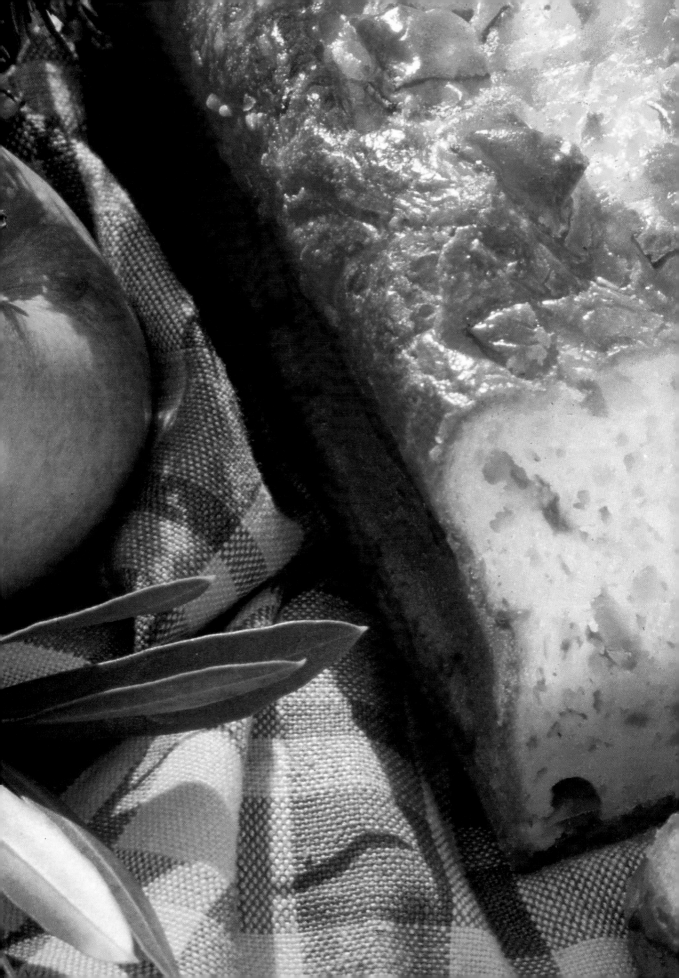

Apple-Pistachio Pound Cake

Serves 6 to 8

2 Granny Smith apples

1/2 cup chopped pistachio nuts

2 tablespoons apple liqueur, or apple brandy

3 eggs, separated

3/4 cup granulated sugar

3/4 cup plus 1 tablespoon all-purpose flour, sifted

1 teaspoon baking powder

1 stick plus 1 tablespoon (9 tablespooons) salted butter, melted

Fine sea salt

1. Preheat the oven to 350°F. Butter and flour an 8 1/2-by-4 1/2-inch loaf pan and set aside. Peel and core the apples, then dice small. In a bowl, combine the apples, pistachio nuts and the apple liqueur, stir to combine, then set aside.

2. In the bowl of an electric mixer, combine the egg yolks with the sugar and beat until creamy and pale yellow. Add the flour and the baking powder and beat to blend. Gradually add the melted butter, beating until batter is smooth. Add the apple mixture and stir to incorporate, then set aside.

3. In the bowl of an electric mixer, combine the egg whites with a pinch of salt and beat until the whites form firm, but not stiff, peaks. Add about 1 cup of the egg whites to the batter and gently fold in. Add the remaining egg whites to the batter and gently fold in, working carefully to maintain as much volume as possible.

4. Scrape the batter into the loaf pan and bake in the center of the oven for 45 to 55 minutes, until a toothpick inserted into the center comes out clean. Transfer the pan to a wire rack and let cool for about 15 minutes, then slide a thin knife around the cake, invert and remove from the pan. Return the cake right side up to the wire rack to cool completely. Serve at room temperature.

Spice Cake with Cashews

Serves 6 to 8

1 stick plus 1 tablespoon (9 tablespoons) butter, softened

1 cup confectioners' sugar

3 large eggs

1 cup plus 3 tablespoons all-purpose flour

1 3/4 teaspoons baking powder

1 teaspoon pumpkin pie spice
(or 1/4 teaspoon each cinnamon, ginger, nutmeg, and allspice)

1 cup freeze-dried banana slices, coarsely chopped

1/2 cup chopped cashew nuts

1 tablespoon Grand Marnier liqueur

1. Preheat the oven to 450°F. In the bowl of an electric mixer, cream the butter and the sugar. Add the eggs one by one, beating after each, then add the flour, baking powder, and spices and beat to blend well, until all lumps are gone. In a bowl, combine the bananas and the nuts, then add to the batter and stir to evenly incorporate.

2. Scrape the batter into an ungreased 8 1/2-by-4 1/2-inch loaf pan, and bake in the center of the oven for 5 minutes, then reduce the temperature to 350°F and bake 40 to 50 minutes, until a toothpick inserted into the center comes out clean. Transfer the pan to a wire rack, sprinkle with the Grand Marnier, then set aside to cool for about 15 minutes. Slide a thin knife around the cake to detach, invert and remove from the pan. Return the cake right side up to the wire rack to cool completely. Serve at room temperature.

57

SOPHIE'S SWEET AND SAVORY LOAVES

Apricot Pound Cake

Serves 6 to 8

1 1/4 cups plus 1 tablespoon granulated sugar

1/2 pound fresh apricots, pitted and chopped into small pieces

3 large eggs

1 cup plus 3 tablespoons all-purpose flour, sifted

3/4 teaspoons baking powder

1 stick plus 3 tablespoons (11 tablespoons) salted butter, melted

1/3 cup sliced almonds

1. Butter and flour an 8 1/2-by-4 1/2-inch loaf pan and set aside. In a saucepan, combine 1/2 cup water and 1/2 cup of the sugar, and bring to a boil over medium-high heat, stirring to dissolve. When the mixture begins to thicken, add the apricots, reduce the heat to low, and simmer for 20 minutes, stirring occasionally. Drain, pat dry with paper towels, and set aside.

2. Preheat the oven to 350°F. In the bowl of an electric mixer, combine the eggs and the remaining 3/4 cup plus 1 tablespoon of granulated sugar and beat until creamy and pale yellow. Add all but 1 tablespoon of the flour, and the baking powder and beat to blend. Gradually add the melted butter, beating constantly to blend smoothly. In a small bowl, combine the reserved apricots with the remaining 1 tablespoon of flour, toss to coat, then add the apricots to the batter, stirring gently to evenly incorporate.

3. Scrape the batter into the loaf pan and garnish with the almonds. Bake in the center of the oven for 40 to 50 minutes, until a toothpick inserted into the center comes out clean. Transfer to a wire rack to cool for about 15 minutes, then slide a thin knife around the cake to detach, invert and remove from the pan. Return the cake right side up to the wire rack and cool completely. Serve at room temperature.

Variation: For Apricot-Banana Pound Cake, reduce the amount of apricots by half, to 1/4 pound, and add 1 ripe thinly-sliced medium banana to the batter.

SOPHIE'S SWEET AND SAVORY LOAVES

Goat Cheese-Zucchini Loaf

Serves 6 to 8

2 tablespoons extra-virgin olive oil

1 medium zucchini, washed and cut into 1/3-inch slices

3 large eggs

1 cup plus 2 tablespoons all-purpose flour, sifted

1 3/4 teaspoons baking powder

Fine sea salt

Freshly ground black pepper

1/3 cup plus 2 tablespoons sunflower oil

1/2 cup milk, hot

1 1/4 cups grated Gruyère cheese

4 ounces goat cheese, cut into small cubes

Leaves from 1 small bunch chervil, chopped

1. Preheat the oven to 350°F. In a skillet, heat the olive oil over medium heat. Add the zucchini and sauté for 15 minutes. Using a slotted spoon, transfer the slices to paper towels to absorb the oil. Discard the oil.

2. In the bowl of an electric mixer, combine the eggs, flour, baking powder, and 2 pinches each of salt and pepper and beat to blend. Gradually add the sunflower oil, beating constantly to combine, then add the milk, beating constantly to combine. Add the Gruyère cheese, beat to incorporate, then add the zucchini, goat cheese, and chervil, beating to blend.

3. Scrape the batter into an ungreased 8 1/2- by-4 1/2-inch loaf pan. Bake in the center of the oven for 45 to 55 minutes, until a toothpick inserted into the center comes out clean. Transfer the pan to a wire rack and let cool for at least 15 minutes, then slide a thin knife around the loaf and remove from the pan. Serve warm or at room temperature.

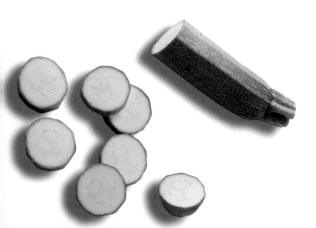

Roasted Pepper, Feta, and Black Olive Loaf

Serves 6 to 8

1/3 cup plus 4 tablespoons extra-virgin olive oil

1 small red bell pepper, roasted, peeled, seeded, and cut into thin strips

1 small green bell pepper, roasted, peeled, seeded, and cut into thin strips

1/3 cup plus 2 tablespoons extra-virgin olive oil

Fine sea salt

Freshly ground black pepper

6 ounces feta cheese, cut into small cubes

2 ounces black olives, split and pits removed

3 large eggs

1 cup plus 2 tablespoons all-purpose flour, sifted

1 3/4 teaspoons baking powder

1/2 cup milk, hot

1 1/4 cups grated Gruyère cheese

1. In a skillet, heat 2 tablespoons of the oil. Add the red and green peppers, a pinch of salt, and 2 pinches of pepper and cook gently over medium-low heat, stirring occasionally, for 45 minutes. Set aside to cool. In a small bowl, combine the feta cheese and olives and set aside.

2. Preheat the oven to 350°F. In the bowl of an electric mixer, combine the eggs, flour, and baking powder and beat to combine. Gradually add the remaining 1/3 cup plus 2 tablespoons oil, beating constantly to blend, then add the milk, beating constantly until blended. Add the Gruyère cheese, stir to combine, then add the pepper and feta mixtures and stir to incorporate.

3. Scrape the batter into an ungreased 8 1/2-by-4 1/2-inch loaf pan. Bake in the center of the oven for 45 to 55 minutes, until a toothpick inserted into the center comes out clean. Transfer the pan to a wire rack and let cool for at least 15 minutes, then slide a thin knife around the loaf and remove from the pan. Serve warm or at room temperature.

61

SOPHIE'S SWEET AND SAVORY LOAVES

Tomato-Candied Ginger Loaf

Serves 6 to 8

1 tablespoon sunflower oil

3 firm, ripe tomatoes, peeled, seeded, and diced

1 stick plus 1 tablespoon (9 tablespoons) salted butter

1 1/2 cups confectioners' sugar

1 large egg

1 large egg yolk

1 1/2 cups all-purpose flour, sifted

1 3/4 teaspoons baking powder

3/8 cup (6 tablespoons) candied ginger, finely chopped

1. In a skillet, combine the oil and tomatoes and sauté over medium-high heat, stirring frequently, until all the liquid has evaporated. Transfer to a bowl, cover, and refrigerate.

2. Preheat the oven to 350°F. In the bowl of an electric mixer, combine the butter and sugar and beat until smooth. Add the whole egg and egg yolk and beat until combined. Add the flour and baking powder, stirring delicately until incorporated. Combine the ginger with the tomatoes, stirring to blend; add them to the batter and stir to incorporate.

3. Scrape the batter into an ungreased 8 1/2-by-4 1/2-inch loaf pan. Bake in the center of the oven for 40 to 50 minutes, until a toothpick inserted into the center comes out clean. Transfer the pan to a wire rack and let cool for at least 15 minutes, then slide a thin knife around the loaf and remove from the pan. Serve at room temperature.

Raspberry Cake

Serves 6 to 8

1 1/4 cups fresh raspberries

6 fresh mint leaves, minced

3 large eggs

3/4 cup plus 2 tablespoons sugar

1 1/4 cups plus 1 tablespoon all-purpose flour, sifted

3/4 teaspoon baking powder

1 stick plus 3 tablespoons (11 tablespoons) salted butter, melted

1 tablespoon raspberry liqueur

1. Preheat the oven to 350°F. Butter and flour an 8 1/2-by-4 1/2-inch loaf pan.
2. In a blender, combine one-third of the raspberries with half of the mint leaves and puree until smooth. Set aside.
3. In the bowl of an electric mixer, combine the eggs and sugar and beat until blended. Add the flour and baking powder, beating until incorporated. Add the melted butter, beating until blended, then add the pureed raspberries and beat to incorporate.
4. Scrape half of the batter into the pan, spreading it in an even layer. Sprinkle the remaining raspberries and mint leaves evenly over the batter, then add the remaining batter. Bake in the center of the oven for 40 to 50 minutes, until a toothpick inserted into the center comes out clean. Remove the pan from the oven and sprinkle on the raspberry liqueur. Transfer to a wire rack and let cool for at least 15 minutes, then slide a thin knife around the loaf and remove from the pan. Serve at room temperature.

*Variation: For Blueberry Cake, omit the raspberries
and use 1 1/4 cups blueberries.*

67

SOPHIE'S SWEET AND
SAVORY LOAVES

Peach-Almond Cake

Serves 6 to 8

1 stick plus 3 tablespoons
(11 tablespoons) salted butter

1 yellow peach, peeled, pitted,
and diced small

1 white peach, peeled, pitted,
and diced small
(or use another yellow peach)

1 nectarine, peeled, pitted,
and diced small

1 3/4 teaspoons vanilla sugar

3 large eggs

3/4 cup plus 2 tablespoons
granulated sugar

1 1/4 cups plus 1 tablespoon
all-purpose flour, sifted

3/4 teaspoon baking powder

1/2 cup sliced almonds,
toasted in a nonstick skillet

1. Preheat the oven to 350°F. In a skillet, heat 1 tablespoon of the butter over medium-low heat. Add the peaches and nectarine, sprinkle on the vanilla sugar, and cook, stirring occasionally, for 15 minutes. Remove from the heat and set aside to cool.

2. Melt the remaining butter. In the bowl of an electric mixer, combine the eggs and granulated sugar and beat until blended. Add the flour and baking powder, beating to incorporate, then add the melted butter and blend. Add the peaches and nectarines and half of the almonds, gently mixing to distribute evenly.

3. Scrape the batter into an ungreased 8 1/2-by-4 1/2-inch loaf pan. Sprinkle on the remaining almonds. Bake in the center of the oven for 40 to 50 minutes, until a toothpick inserted into the center comes out clean. Transfer the pan to a wire rack and let cool for at least 15 minutes, then slide a thin knife around the loaf and remove from the pan. Serve warm or at room temperature.

Variations: : For Apricot-Almond Cake, omit the peaches and replace them with 1/2 pound fresh apricots. For Apricot-Banana-Almond Cake, omit the peaches and replace them with 1/4 pound fresh apricots and 1/4 pound bananas.

68

SOPHIE'S SWEET AND
SAVORY LOAVES

Seafood Loaf

Serves 6 to 8

Fine sea salt

3 ounces mussels

3 ounces cleaned calamari

1 tablespoon plus 1 teaspoon salted butter (or 4 teaspoons)

Freshly ground black pepper

1 clove garlic, minced

1 shallot, peeled and minced

2 sprigs flat-leaf parsley, chopped

3 ounces medium shrimp, peeled, deveined, and cut into 1/2-inch pieces

3 large eggs

1 cup plus 2 tablespoons all-purpose flour, sifted

1 3/4 teaspoons baking powder

1/3 cup plus 2 tablespoons sunflower oil

1/2 cup milk, hot

1 1/4 cups grated Gruyère cheese

1. Preheat the oven to 350°F. Bring a pot of salted water to a boil, drop in the mussels and cook for 20 seconds. Using a slotted spoon, remove them and take the meat out of the shells. Slice the calamari crosswise into thin rings. In a saucepan, melt the butter over medium-high heat. Add the mussels and calamari and sauté, stirring frequently, for 3 minutes. Add 2 pinches each of salt and pepper, the garlic, and shallot and cook for an additional 2 minutes, stirring often. Remove from the heat, sprinkle on the parsley, stir to blend, add the shrimp, and stir to incorporate. Set aside.

2. In the bowl of an electric mixer, combine the eggs, flour, and baking powder and beat to combine. Gradually add the oil, beating constantly to blend, then add the milk, beating constantly to blend. Add the cheese, stir to blend, then add the mixture to the shellfish mixture, stirring to incorporate.

3. Scrape the batter into an ungreased 8 1/2-by-4 1/2-inch loaf pan. Bake in the center of the oven for 45 to 55 minutes, until a toothpick inserted into the center comes out clean. Transfer the pan to a wire rack and let cool for at least 15 minutes, then slide a thin knife around the loaf and remove from the pan. Serve warm or at room temperature.

Tomato-Mozzarella-Basil Loaf

Serves 6 to 8

2 firm, ripe tomatoes

1 tablespoon extra-virgin olive oil

Fine sea salt

Freshly ground black pepper

7 ounces mozzarella cheese, diced medium

8 leaves fresh basil

3 large eggs

1 cup plus 2 tablespoons all-purpose flour, sifted

1 3/4 teaspoons baking powder

1/3 cup plus 2 tablespoons sunflower oil

1/2 cup milk, hot

1 1/4 cups grated Gruyère cheese

1. Preheat the oven to 350°F. Bring a small saucepan of water to a boil. Add the tomatoes and cook for 30 seconds. Remove with a slotted spoon, peel and seed them, then chop them into small pieces. In a skillet, heat the olive oil over medium-high heat. Add the tomatoes and 2 pinches each of salt and pepper, and cook until the liquid has evaporated, stirring frequently. Remove from the heat and set aside to cool. Add the mozzarella and basil and stir to incorporate.

2. In the bowl of an electric mixer, combine the eggs, flour, and baking powder and beat until smooth. Gradually add the oil, beating constantly to blend, then add the milk, beating constantly to blend. Add the cheese, beating to incorporate. Add the tomato mixture to the batter and beat to combine.

3. Scrape the batter into an ungreased 8 1/2-by-4 1/2-inch loaf pan. Bake in the center of the oven for 45 to 55 minutes, until a toothpick inserted into the center comes out clean. Transfer the pan to a wire rack and let cool for at least 15 minutes, then slide a thin knife around the loaf and remove from the pan. Serve warm or at room temperature.

71

SOPHIE'S SWEET AND SAVORY LOAVES

Smoked Salmon and Herring Loaf

Serves 6 to 8

3 large eggs

1 cup plus 2 tablespoons all-purpose flour, sifted

1 3/4 teaspoons baking powder

1/3 cup plus 2 tablespoons sunflower oil

1/2 cup milk, hot

Leaves from 1 sprig dill

Freshly ground black pepper

1 1/4 cups grated Gruyère cheese

6 ounces sliced smoked salmon, cut into thin strips

2 ounces marinated herring, drained and cut into thin strips

1 teaspoon grated horseradish

1. Preheat the oven to 350°F. In the bowl of an electric mixer, combine the eggs, flour, and baking powder and beat to combine. Gradually add the oil, beating constantly to blend, then add the milk, beating constantly to blend. Add the dill and 2 pinches of pepper and beat to blend. Add the cheese and beat to incorporate. Add the salmon and herring, beat to blend, then add the horseradish and blend.

2. Scrape the batter into an ungreased 8 1/2-by-4 1/2-inch loaf pan. Bake in the center of the oven for 45 to 55 minutes, until a toothpick inserted into the center comes out clean. Transfer the pan to a wire rack and let cool for at least 15 minutes, then slide a thin knife around the loaf and remove from the pan. Serve warm or at room temperature.

Lemon Cake

Serves 6 to 8

3 large eggs

3/4 plus 2 tablespoons sugar

1 1/4 cups plus 1 tablespoon all-purpose flour, sifted

3/4 teaspoon baking powder

1 stick plus 3 tablespoons (11 tablespoons) salted butter, melted

2 lemons

1. Preheat the oven to 350°F. Butter and flour an 8 1/2-by-4 1/2-inch loaf pan.
2. In the bowl of an electric mixer, combine the eggs and sugar and beat until light in color. Add the flour and baking powder, beating until smooth. Pour in the melted butter and mix until incorporated. Set the batter aside.
3. Bring a small saucepan of water to a boil. Wash the lemons, remove the zest in long strips, then drop the zest into the boiling water for 5 seconds, drain, plunge the zest into ice water, drain again, and blot dry on paper towels. Squeeze the juice from the lemons and add it, along with the zest, to the batter. Using a rubber spatula, gently fold the juice and zest into the batter until blended.
4. Scrape the batter into the pan. Bake in the center of the oven for 40 to 50 minutes, until a toothpick inserted into the center comes out clean. Transfer the pan to a wire rack and let cool for at least 15 minutes, then slide a thin knife around the loaf and remove from the pan. Serve warm or at room temperature.

*Variations: For Lemon-Lime Cake, instead of using 2 lemons,
use one lemon and one lime. For Grapefruit Cake, instead of using lemons,
substitute the juice of 1/2 grapefruit in the batter.*

Normandy Cake

Serves 6 to 8

1 Golden Delicious apple, peeled and grated

4 ounces fresh red currants

1/2 teaspoon freshly grated nutmeg

2 tablespoons Calvados, or apple brandy

3 large eggs, separated

3/4 cup sugar

3/4 cup all-purpose flour, sifted

1 teaspoon baking powder

1 stick plus 1 1/2 tablespoons (9 1/2 tablespoons) salted butter, melted

1 tablespoon crème fraîche

1. Preheat the oven to 350°F. Butter and flour an 8 1/2-by-4 1/2-inch loaf pan. In a small bowl, combine the apple, currants, nutmeg, and Calvados. Set aside.

2. In the bowl of an electric mixer, combine the egg yolks and sugar and beat until light in color. Add the flour and baking powder, beating constantly until blended; add the melted butter and beat to blend, then add the crème fraîche and beat to incorporate. Strain the apple-currant mixture, setting aside the liquid. Add the apples and currants to the batter and beat to blend.

3. In a medium bowl, beat the egg whites until they hold stiff peaks. Add them to the batter, working carefully while folding them to maintain as much volume as possible.

4. Scrape the batter into the pan. Bake in the center of the oven for 45 to 55 minutes, until a toothpick inserted into the center comes out clean. Remove the pan from the oven, sprinkle on the reserved liquid, transfer to a wire rack and let cool for at least 15 minutes, then slide a thin knife around the loaf and remove from the pan. Serve warm or at room temperature.

SOPHIE'S SWEET AND SAVORY LOAVES

Pineapple-Rum Cake

Serves 6 to 8

1/2 pineapple, peeled, cored, and cut into 1/2-inch cubes

2 tablespoons dark or light rum

3 large eggs

1 1/4 cups plus 1 tablespoon all-purpose flour, sifted

3/4 teaspoon baking powder

1 stick plus 3 tablespoons (11 tablespoons) salted butter, melted

1. Preheat the oven to 350°F. Butter and flour an 8 1/2-by-4 1/2-inch loaf pan. In a nonreactive bowl, combine the pineapple and 1 tablespoon of the rum and set aside.
2. In the bowl of an electric mixer, combine the eggs, flour, and baking powder, and beat until smooth, then add the melted butter and beat until blended.
3. Drain the pineapple pieces and puree half of them in an electric mixer until smooth. Add to the batter, beating to incorporate; add the remaining pieces to the batter, gently mixing to distribute.
4. Scrape the batter into the pan. Bake in the center of the oven for 45 to 55 minutes, until a toothpick inserted into the center comes out clean. Remove the pan from the oven, sprinkle on the remaining 1 tablespoon rum, then transfer to a wire rack and let cool for at least 15 minutes. Slide a thin knife around the loaf and remove from the pan. Serve warm or at room temperature.

79

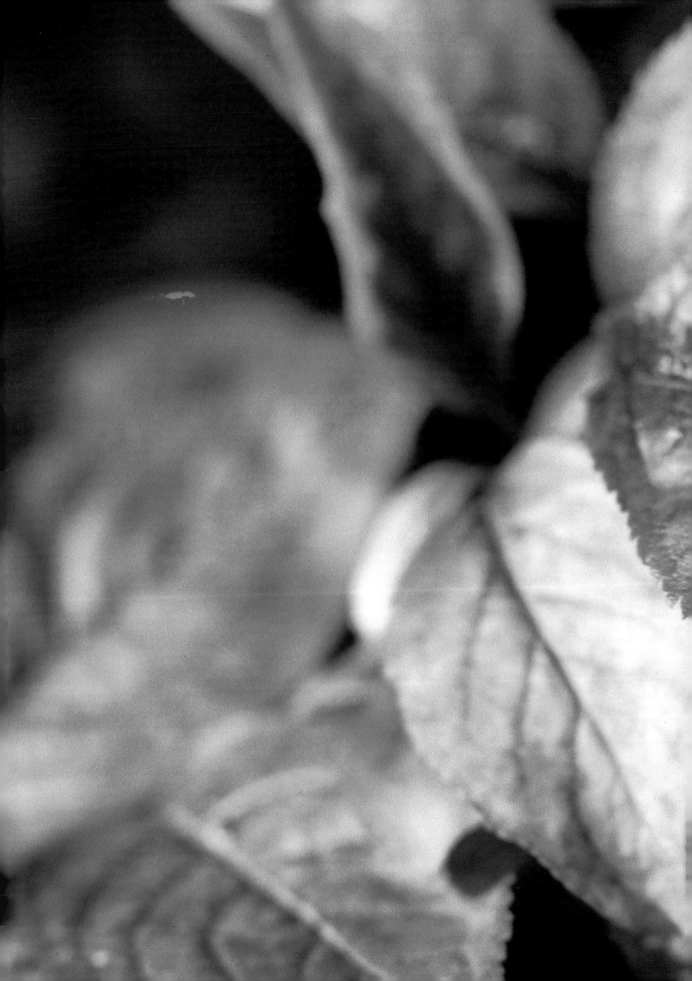

Autumn

Cheddar, Ham, Beer, and Mustard Loaf

Serves 6 to 8

3 tablespoons light beer

1 teaspoon strong Dijon mustard

Fine sea salt

Freshly ground black pepper

1/3 pound boiled ham, cut into small pieces

2 ounces cheddar cheese, cut into small pieces

3 large eggs

1 cup all-purpose flour, sifted

3/4 teaspoon baking powder

1/3 cup plus 2 tablespoons sunflower oil

1/2 cup milk, hot

1 1/4 cups grated Gruyère cheese

82

1. In a small bowl, combine the beer, mustard, and 2 pinches each of salt and pepper and beat to blend. Add the ham and cheddar, turn to coat evenly, and set aside for 30 minutes.
2. Preheat the oven to 350°F. In the bowl of an electric mixer, combine the eggs, flour, and baking powder and beat until well blended and smooth. Gradually add the oil, beating constantly to blend. Gradually add the milk, beating constantly to blend. Mix in the Gruyère with a wooden spoon, then add the ham-cheddar mixture, stirring until incorporated.
3. Scrape the batter into an ungreased 8 1/2-by-4 1/2-inch loaf pan. Bake in the middle of the oven for 45 to 55 minutes, until a toothpick inserted into the center comes out clean. Transfer to a wire rack and let cool for at least 15 minutes, then slide a thin knife around the loaf and remove from the pan. Serve warm or at room temperature.

*Variation: For a Ham, Gouda, and Cumin Loaf,
omit the cheddar and add 2 ounces chopped Gouda cheese and
a pinch of cumin seeds to the batter.*

Ratatouille Loaf

Serves 6 to 8

1/2 large onion

1 firm, ripe tomato

1/2 medium eggplant

1/2 medium zucchini

1/3 cup plus 2 tablespoons extra-virgin olive oil

Fine sea salt

Freshly ground black pepper

3 basil leaves, chopped

Leaves from 1 small bunch chervil, chopped

3 large eggs

1 cup all-purpose flour, sifted

1 3/4 teaspoons baking powder

1/2 cup milk, hot

1 1/4 cups grated Gruyère cheese

1. Peel and cut all of the vegetables into medium dice. In a large skillet, heat 2 tablespoons oil over medium-high heat. Sauté the onion, stirring frequently, until lightly colored, about 4 minutes. Add the tomato, eggplant, zucchini, and 2 pinches each of salt and pepper and simmer for about 20 minutes, stirring occasionally. Set aside to cool, then sprinkle with the basil and chervil.

2. Preheat the oven to 350°F. In the bowl of an electric mixer, beat the eggs, flour, and baking powder together until smooth. Gradually add the remaining 1/3 cup oil, beating constantly to blend, then gradually add the milk, beating constantly to blend. Add the cheese, mix, then gently stir in the vegetable mixture.

3. Scrape the batter into an ungreased 8 1/2-by-4 1/2-inch pan. Bake in the middle of the oven for 45 to 55 minutes, until a toothpick inserted into the center comes out clean. Transfer to a wire rack and let cool for at least 15 minutes, then slide a thin knife around the loaf and remove from the pan. Serve warm or at room temperature.

Mushroom Loaf

Serves 6 to 8

1/3 cup plus 2 tablespoons sunflower oil

1/2 pound cultivated white mushrooms, stems removed and discarded, wiped and finely chopped

Fine sea salt

Freshly ground black pepper

1 clove garlic, crushed

Leaves from 1 small bunch flat-leaf parsley, chopped

7 tablespoons salted butter, softened

3 large eggs

1 1/3 cups all-purpose flour, sifted

1 3/4 teaspoons baking powder

1 1/4 cups grated Gruyère cheese

1. Preheat the oven to 350°F. In a skillet, heat 3 tablespoons oil over medium-high heat and cook the mushrooms until all the liquid has evaporated. Season with 2 pinches each of salt and pepper, add the garlic and parsley, and stir to combine. Set aside to cool.
2. In the bowl of an electric mixer, combine the butter and the remaining oil and beat until smooth. One at a time, add the eggs, beating until incorporated. Add the flour and baking powder and beat to blend. Add the cheese, stir to combine, then add the mushrooms and stir to combine.
3. Scrape the batter into an ungreased 8 1/2-by-4 1/2-inch loaf pan. Bake in the middle of the oven for 45 to 55 minutes, until a toothpick inserted into the center comes out clean. Transfer to a wire rack and let cool for at least 15 minutes, then slide a thin knife around the loaf and remove from the pan. Serve warm or at room temperature.

Variation: Depending on the season,
you can use other kinds of mushrooms, such as wild mushrooms
(porcini or chanterelles) in the fall.

85

SOPHIE'S SWEET AND
SAVORY LOAVES

Pear Cake

Serves 6 to 8

1 1/4 cups plus 2 tablespoons sugar

2 Bartlett pears, peeled, halved lengthwise, and cored

3 large eggs

3/4 cup plus 2 tablespoons granulated sugar

1 cup plus 3 tablespoons all-purpose flour, sifted

3/4 teaspoon baking powder

1 stick plus 3 tablespoons (11 tablespoons) salted butter, melted

1. Preheat the oven to 350°F. Butter and flour an 8 1/2-by-4 1/2-inch loaf pan. Combine 1/2 cup sugar and 3 ounces water in a small skillet and bring to a boil over high heat. Cook, stirring constantly, until the sugar dissolves. Reduce the heat to low. Add the pears to the simmering syrup and poach until just tender, about 10 to 15 minutes. Remove with a slotted spoon and cut into 3/4-inch cubes. Set aside.

2. In the bowl of an electric mixer, combine the eggs and the remaining sugar and beat until smooth. Add all but 1 tablespoon of the flour, and the baking powder, and beat until smooth. Add the melted butter and beat to incorporate. Sprinkle the pears with the remaining 1 tablespoon flour, turning to coat them evenly, then add to the batter and stir to combine.

3. Scrape the batter into the pan. Bake in the center of the oven for 40 to 50 minutes, until a toothpick inserted into the center comes out clean. Transfer to a wire rack and let cool for at least 15 minutes, then slide a thin knife around the loaf and remove from the pan. Serve at room temperature.

Variation: For Pear and Chocolate Chip Cake,
add 1/4 cup chocolate chips to the batter. For Pear and Almond Cake,
add 1/3 cup ground almonds and 2 tablespoons toasted
slivered almonds to the batter.

Spiced Banana-Fig Bread

Serves 6 to 8

1 3/4 to 2 cups whole wheat flour

1 cup heather, buckwheat, or other flavored honey, plus additional for glazing

1/4 cup sugar

1 teaspoon baking powder

Pinch of baking soda

5 pieces star anise, finely ground

Pinch of ground cinnamon

Pinch of ground cloves

2 ounces dried sliced bananas, cut into small pieces

2 ounces dried figs, cut into small pieces

1. In a large mixing bowl, combine 1 3/4 cups flour and the honey and stir until well blended, adding a little more flour if the mixture is runny. Let stand for 1 hour, then add the sugar, baking powder, baking soda, and the spices and knead well to incorporate.

2. Preheat the oven to 350°F. Butter and flour an 8 1/2-by-4 1/2-inch loaf pan. Add the bananas and figs to the flour mixture and knead with your hands until evenly incorporated.

3. Scrape the batter into the loaf pan. Bake in the middle of the oven for 50 to 60 minutes, until a toothpick inserted into the center comes out clean. After removing the bread from the oven, brush with a little honey. Transfer to a wire rack and let cool for at least 15 minutes, then slide a thin knife around the loaf and remove from the pan. Serve at room temperature.

Plum Cake

Serves 6 to 8

2 tablespoons salted butter, chilled

1 tablespoon plum liqueur

1/2 pound ripe red plums, halved and pitted

3 large eggs

3/4 cup plus 2 tablespoons sugar

1 stick plus 1 tablespoon (9 tablespoons) salted butter, melted

1 cup plus 2 tablespoons all-purpose flour, sifted

3/4 teaspoon baking powder

1. Preheat the oven to 350°F. Butter and flour an 8 1/2-by-4 1/2-inch loaf pan. Melt 2 tablespoons of the butter in a medium skillet over low heat. Add the plum liqueur, stir to combine, then add the plums, cut side down, and cook for 8 to 10 minutes over low heat until lightly browned and tender. Set aside to cool.

2. In the bowl of an electric mixer, beat the eggs and sugar until smooth. Add all but 1 tablespoon of the flour and the baking powder, and stir to blend. Add the melted butter and beat to blend. Using a slotted spoon, transfer the plums to a small bowl; reserve the liquid.

3. Sprinkle the plums with the remaining 1 tablespoon flour, turning to coat lightly, then add the plums to the batter and gently fold until evenly distributed.

4. Scrape the batter into the pan. Bake in the middle of the oven for 40 to 50 minutes, until a toothpick inserted into the center comes out clean. Transfer the pan to a wire rack, then sprinkle with the reserved plum liquid. Let cool for 15 minutes, then slide a thin knife around the cake and remove from the pan. Serve at room temperature.

Variation: : You can replace red plums with other plum varieties,
such as yellow golden-gage or little mirabelles.

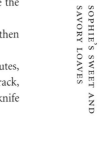

91

SOPHIE'S SWEET AND
SAVORY LOAVES

Goat Cheese, Walnut, and Currant Loaf

Serves 6 to 8

3 large eggs

1 cup plus 2 tablespoons all-purpose flour, sifted

3/4 teaspoon baking powder

Fine sea salt

Freshly ground black pepper

1/3 cup plus 2 tablespoons sunflower oil

1/2 cup milk, hot

1 1/4 cups grated Gruyère cheese

7-ounce log goat cheese, crumbled into small pieces

1/3 cup currants, plumped in warm water and drained

1/4 cup finely chopped walnuts

1. Preheat the oven to 350°F. In the bowl of an electric mixer, combine the eggs, flour, baking powder, and a pinch each of salt and pepper and beat until well blended. Gradually add the oil, beating constantly to blend. Gradually add the milk, beating constantly to blend. Add the Gruyère, stir to combine, then add the goat cheese, currants, and nuts and stir to combine.

2. Scrape the batter into an ungreased 8 1/2-by-4 1/2-inch loaf pan. Bake in the center of the oven for 45 to 55 minutes, until a toothpick inserted into the center comes out clean. Transfer the pan to a wire rack and let cool for at least 15 minutes, then slide a thin knife around the loaf and remove from the pan. Serve warm or at room temperature.

Carrot Cake

Serves 6 to 8

1 tablespoon salted butter for the pan

3 large eggs

1 cup sugar

3/4 cup plus 2 tablespoons sunflower oil

2 teaspoons ground cinnamon

Freshly grated nutmeg

2 3/4 cups all-purpose flour, sifted

1 3/4 teaspoons baking powder

14 ounces carrots (about 5 or 6 medium carrots), peeled and finely grated

2/3 cup currants, plumped in warm water and drained

1.   Preheat the oven to 350°F. Butter and flour an 8 1/2-by-4 1/2-inch loaf pan. In the bowl of an electric mixer, beat the eggs and sugar together until it has doubled in volume. Add the oil, the cinnamon, and a pinch of nutmeg and beat until smooth. Add the flour and baking powder, beat to blend, then gently fold in the carrots and currants.

2.   Scrape the batter into the pan. Bake in the center of the oven for 45 to 55 minutes, until a toothpick inserted into the center comes out clean. Transfer the pan to a wire rack and let cool for at least 15 minutes, then slide a thin knife around the loaf and remove from the pan. Serve at room temperature.

Variation: : For Pumpkin Cake, omit the carrots.
Instead, peel and chop 14 ounces pumpkin into medium chunks and
place in a saucepan. Cover with milk and cook over low heat for
about 20 minutes, until tender. Drain well and
mash until smooth. Add to the batter.

Banana-Bacon Loaf

Serves 6 to 8

6 ounces thin-sliced bacon, finely chopped

1 banana, cut into 1/3-inch slices

1 teaspoon freshly grated ginger

Fine sea salt

Freshly ground black pepper

2 tablespoons chopped toasted peanuts

3 large eggs

1 cup plus 2 tablespoons all-purpose flour, sifted

1 3/4 teaspoons baking powder

1/3 cup sunflower oil

1/2 cup milk, hot

1 1/4 cups grated Gruyère cheese

1. Preheat the oven to 350°F. In a large skillet, cook the bacon over medium heat for 2 minutes. Remove from the heat and stir in the banana, ginger, a pinch each of salt and pepper, and the peanuts. Set aside.

2. In the bowl of an electric mixer, beat the eggs, flour, and baking powder together until smooth. Gradually add the oil, beating constantly to blend. Gradually add the milk, beating constantly to blend. Add the cheese, stir to combine, then add the bacon-banana mixture and stir to combine.

3. Scrape the batter into an ungreased 8 1/2-by-4 1/2-inch loaf pan. Bake in the center of the oven for 45 to 55 minutes, until a toothpick inserted into the center comes out clean. Transfer the pan to a wire rack and let cool for at least 15 minutes, then slide a thin knife around the loaf and remove from the pan. Serve warm or at room temperature.

Asparagus-Chanterelles Loaf

Serves 6 to 8

5 ounces tender green asparagus, coarse ends snapped off	1/2 teaspoon ground coriander
Fine sea salt	3 large eggs
1/4 pound fresh chanterelles	1 cup plus 2 tablespoons all-purpose flour, sifted
Freshly ground black pepper	1 3/4 teaspoons baking powder
2 tablespoons salted butter	1/3 cup plus 2 tablespoons sunflower oil
1 shallot, finely chopped	1/2 cup milk, hot
1 teaspoon fresh thyme leaves	1 1/2 cups grated Gruyère cheese

1. Preheat the oven to 350°F. Peel the asparagus from the tip to the end. Cook them in salted boiling water until tender, about 2 minutes. Remove, drain on paper towels, then cut into 1-inch pieces and set aside.

2. Quickly rinse the chanterelles under cold running water, then drain and blot dry on paper towels. Season with 2 pinches each of salt and pepper. Melt the butter in a large skillet, add the chanterelles, and sauté over medium-high heat, stirring frequently, for 3 minutes. Add the shallot, thyme, and coriander and, stirring frequently, cook for 1 minute, then remove from the heat. Add the asparagus, stir to combine, and set aside.

3. In the bowl of an electric mixer, combine the eggs, flour, and baking powder and beat until smooth. Gradually add the oil, stirring constantly until blended. Gradually add the milk, stirring constantly until blended. Add the cheese, stir to combine, then add the mushroom-asparagus mixture and stir to combine.

4. Scrape the batter into an ungreased 8 1/2-by-4 1/2-inch loaf pan. Bake in the center of the oven for 45 to 55 minutes, until a toothpick inserted into the center comes out clean. Transfer the pan to a wire rack and let cool for at least 15 minutes, then slide a thin knife around the loaf and remove from the pan. Serve warm or at room temperature.

Chicken Liver and Pine Nut Loaf

Serves 6 to 8

2 tablespoons salted butter

1 shallot, finely chopped

1/2 pound chicken livers, cleaned

Fine sea salt

Freshly ground black pepper

1 tablespoon medium port

1/4 cup pine nuts

3 basil leaves, finely chopped

2 mint leaves, finely chopped

3 large eggs

1 cup plus 2 tablespoons
all-purpose flour, sifted

1 3/4 teaspoons baking powder

1/3 cup plus 2 tablespoons sunflower oil

1/2 cup milk, hot

1 1/4 cups grated Gruyère cheese

1. Preheat the oven to 350°F. In a skillet, melt the butter over medium-high heat. Add the shallot and sauté until softened, about 4 minutes. Add the chicken livers and 2 pinches each of salt and pepper and cook for 5 minutes, stirring frequently, until the livers are lightly browned. Add the port and cook over medium heat, stirring occasionally, until the liquid has evaporated. Remove from the heat and add the pine nuts, basil, and mint, stir to combine. Set aside.

2. In the bowl of an electric mixer, combine the eggs, flour, and baking powder and beat together until smooth. Gradually beat in the oil, stirring constantly to blend. Gradually beat in the milk, stirring constantly to blend. Add the cheese and stir to combine. Add the chicken liver mixture and stir to combine.

3. Scrape the batter into an ungreased 8 1/2-by-4 1/2-inch loaf pan. Bake in the center of the oven for 45 to 55 minutes, until a toothpick inserted into the center comes out clean. Transfer the pan to a wire rack and let cool for at least 15 minutes, then slide a thin knife around the loaf and remove from the pan. Serve warm or at room temperature.

Three-Cheese Loaf

Serves 6 to 8

3 large eggs

1 cup plus 2 tablespoons all-purpose flour, sifted

1 3/4 teaspoons baking powder

Freshly ground black pepper

1/3 cup plus 2 tablespoons sunflower oil

1/2 cup milk, hot

1 1/4 cups grated Gruyère cheese

1/4 pound bleu d'Auvergne, or other blue cheese,
such as Maytag Blue or Roquefort, crumbled

1/4 pound mimolette, or Gouda or Edam cheese, diced small

1. Preheat the oven to 350°F. In the bowl of an electric mixer, combine the eggs, flour, baking powder, and 2 pinches of pepper and beat until blended. Gradually add the oil, beating constantly until blended. Gradually add the milk, beating until blended. Stir in the Gruyère. Using a rubber spatula, gently fold in the blue and mimolette cheeses.

2. Scrape the batter into an ungreased 8 1/2-by-4 1/2-inch loaf pan. Bake in the center of the oven for 45 to 55 minutes, until a toothpick inserted into the center comes out clean. Transfer the pan to a wire rack and let cool for at least 15 minutes, then slide a thin knife around the loaf and remove from the pan. Serve warm or at room temperature.

101

SOPHIE'S SWEET AND
SAVORY LOAVES

Apple-Cinnamon Cake

Serves 6 to 8

3 large eggs

3/4 cup plus 2 tablespoons sugar

1 cup plus 2 tablespoons all-purpose flour, sifted

3/4 teaspoon baking powder

Ground cinnamon

1 stick plus 3 tablespoons (11 tablespoons) salted butter, melted

1 Golden Delicious apple

1. Preheat the oven to 350°F. Butter and flour an 8 1/2-by-4 1/2-inch loaf pan. In the bowl of an electric mixer, combine the eggs and sugar and beat to blend. Add the flour, baking powder, and a pinch of cinnamon and beat to blend. Add the melted butter and beat to blend. Peel the apple and grate it over the batter; stir to incorporate evenly.

2. Scrape the batter into the pan. Bake in the center of the oven for 40 to 50 minutes, until a toothpick inserted into the center comes out clean. Transfer the pan to a wire rack and let cool for at least 15 minutes, then slide a thin knife around the loaf and remove from the pan. Serve at room temperature.

Variations: For Apple, Cinnamon, and Raisin Cake,
*add 1/4 cup raisins that have been plumped in warm water and drained
to the batter. For Granny Smith and Calvados Cake, replace the Golden Delicious
apple with a Granny Smith apple. After removing the cake from the oven, sprinkle
on 1 tablespoon Calvados. For Apple Compote Cake, peel and dice the apple.
Cook with 1 tablespoon melted butter over medium heat. Sprinkle
with 1 tablespoon sugar, stirring until it dissolves.
Chill before adding the apples to the batter.*

Bratwurst-Apple Loaf

Serves 6 to 8

1 pippin apple, or other firm, tangy apple

2 tablespoons salted butter

7 ounces bratwurst, cut into individual links

1 tablespoon crème fraîche or sour cream

Fine sea salt

Freshly ground black pepper

3 large eggs

1 cup plus 2 tablespoons all-purpose flour, sifted

1 3/4 teaspoons baking powder

1/3 cup plus 2 tablespoons sunflower oil

1/2 cup milk, hot

1 1/4 cups grated Gruyère cheese

1. Peel and cut the apple into 1/2-inch cubes. Combine 1 tablespoon butter and 3 tablespoons water in a skillet. Add the apples and cook, stirring frequently, over low heat for 15 minutes, until lightly browned, turning occasionally. Set aside.

2. Preheat the oven to 350°F. Add the remaining 1 tablespoon butter to a skillet and cook the sausages over medium-high heat for 5 minutes, turning often. Remove the sausage casings, chop the filling into small pieces and mix with the apples. Add the crème fraîche and two pinches of both the salt and pepper.

3. In the bowl of an electric mixer, combine the eggs, flour, and baking powder and beat until well blended. Gradually add the oil, beating constantly to blend. Gradually add the milk, beating constantly to blend. Add the cheese, stir to combine, then add the sausage-apple mixture, and stir to combine.

4. Scrape the batter into an ungreased 8 1/2-by-4 1/2-inch loaf pan and bake in the center of the oven for 45 to 55 minutes, until a toothpick inserted into the center comes out clean. Transfer the pan to a wire rack and let cool for at least 15 minutes, then slide a thin knife around the loaf and remove from the pan. Serve warm or at room temperature.

Potato-Zucchini Loaf

Serves 6 to 8

2 medium zucchini

2 tablespoons sunflower oil

2 medium red skinned potatoes

2 cups heavy cream

3 tablespoons salted butter

Fine sea salt

Freshly ground black pepper

Pinch of freshly grated nutmeg

3/4 cup all-purpose flour, sifted

8 large eggs (5 large eggs, 3 large egg yolks, 3 large egg whites)

1 1/4 cups (2 1/2 ounces) grated Gruyère cheese

1 tablespoon chopped parsley

1 tablespoon chopped chervil

1. Butter and flour an 8 1/2-by-4 1/2-inch loaf pan. Bring a large pot of water to a boil, then keep it at a simmer on a back burner. Meanwhile, peel the zucchini lengthwise, leaving several narrow strips on each zucchini to form a decorative design. Cut crosswise into thin slices. Heat 1 tablespoon oil in a skillet over medium-high heat. Add the zucchini and cook for 5 minutes, turning occasionally. Remove from the pan, transfer to a bowl and set aside to cool.

2. Preheat the oven to 350°F. Peel and dice the potatoes. Heat the remaining tablespoon of oil in the skillet and sauté the potatoes until lightly colored, about 5 to 7 minutes. Remove from the heat and add to the bowl with the reserved zucchini. In the skillet, bring the cream, butter, 2 pinches each of salt and pepper, and nutmeg to a boil over medium-high heat. Add the flour, whisk to combine, then cook over medium heat, stirring occasionally, until the mixture thickens. Remove from the heat, whisk in the egg yolks then the whole eggs; add the Gruyère, parsley, and chervil, and stir to combine. Pour the thickened cream over the vegetables.

3. In the bowl of an electric mixer, beat the egg whites until they form stiff peaks. Using a rubber spatula, gently fold them into the mixture, carefully working to maintain as much volume as possible.

4. Scrape the batter into the pan. Set the pan into another, larger baking pan and fill this second pan halfway with boiling water. Bake in the center of the oven for 45 to 55 minutes, until a toothpick inserted into the center comes out clean. Transfer the pan to a wire rack and let cool for at least 15 minutes, then slide a thin knife around the loaf and remove from the pan. Serve warm or at room temperature.

SOPHIE'S SWEET AND SAVORY LOAVES

Exotic Pound Cake

Serves 6 to 8

3 ounces candied pineapple, diced

3 ounces candied papayas, diced

3 ounces candied apricots, diced

1 cup plus 3 tablespoons all-purpose flour, sifted

1 vanilla bean, split lengthwise, seeds scraped out; pod reserved for another use

1 stick plus 1 tablespoon (9 tablespoons) salted butter, slightly softened

1 cup confectioners' sugar

3 large eggs

1/2 teaspoon baking powder

2 tablespoons light rum

1. Preheat the oven to 450°F. In a mixing bowl, combine the pineapple, papayas, and apricots with 1 tablespoon flour to coat. Sprinkle with the vanilla seeds and mix.

2. In the bowl of an electric mixer, cream the butter and sugar until light and fluffy. One at a time, stir in the eggs. Add the remaining flour and the baking powder and mix until smooth. Using a rubber spatula, gently fold in the fruits.

3. Scrape the batter into an 8 1/2-by-4 1/2-inch loaf pan. Bake in the center of the oven for 5 minutes, then lower the heat to 350°F, and continue baking for 40 to 50 minutes more, until a toothpick inserted into the center comes out clean. Remove from the oven, sprinkle with the rum, transfer to a wire rack, and let cool for at least 15 minutes, then slide a thin knife around the loaf and remove from the pan. Serve at room temperature.

Variation: : *For Date and Fig Cake, omit the pineapple, apricots, and papayas. Dust 2/3 cup each of diced dried dates and dried figs with flour. Stir them into the batter.*

110

SOPHIE'S SWEET AND SAVORY LOAVES

Maple-Pecan Cake

Serves 6 to 8

1 stick plus 1 tablespoon (9 tablespoons) salted butter

1/2 cup plus 2 tablespoons sugar

3 large eggs

Grated zest and juice of 1 lemon

1 cup plus 2 tablespoons all-purpose flour, sifted

1 teaspoon baking powder

2 tablespoons maple syrup

1 cup pecans, coarsely chopped

1. Preheat the oven to 350°F. Butter and flour an 8 1/2-by-4 1/2-inch loaf pan. In the bowl of an electric mixer, cream the butter and sugar until light and fluffy. One at a time, stir in the eggs, then add the lemon zest and juice and mix until smooth. Add the flour, baking powder, and maple syrup and beat until well blended. Add the pecans and stir to combine.
2. Scrape the batter into the pan. Bake in the center of the oven for 45 to 55 minutes, until a toothpick inserted into the center comes out clean. Transfer the pan to a wire rack and let cool for at least 15 minutes, then slide a thin knife around the loaf and remove from the pan. Serve at room temperature.

Nougat Cake

Serves 6 to 8

1 cup confectioners' sugar

1 stick plus 1 tablespoon (9 tablespoons) salted butter, softened

3 large eggs

1 cup plus 2 tablespoons all-purpose flour, sifted

3/4 teaspoon baking powder

1/2 teaspoon almond extract

1/2 teaspoon ground coriander

Pinch of ground anise

6 ounces soft nougat candy with almonds, cut into small squares
with kitchen shears or a small sharp knife

1. Preheat the oven to 450°F. In the bowl of an electric mixer, cream the sugar and butter until light and fluffy. Add the eggs one at a time, beating to blend, then add the flour, baking powder, almond extract, coriander, and anise and beat until blended. Add the nougat and stir to combine.

2. Scrape the batter into an ungreased 8 1/2-by-4 1/2-inch loaf pan. Bake for 5 minutes, then reduce the heat to 350°F, and cook for 45 to 55 minutes, until a toothpick inserted into the center comes out clean. Remove from the oven, invert the pan and immediately unmold. Cool on a wire rack, right side up, before slicing. Serve at room temperature.

113

SOPHIE'S SWEET AND
SAVORY LOAVES

Preserved Tangerine Cake

Serves 6 to 8

1 stick plus 3 tablespoons (11 tablespoons) salted butter, softened

1/2 cup plus 3 tablespoons sugar

3 large eggs

1 1/2 cups plus 2 tablespoons all-purpose flour, sifted

3/4 teaspoon baking powder

2/3 pound preserved tangerines or oranges, cut into small pieces

2 tablespoons Cointreau or other orange liqueur

1. Preheat the oven to 450°F. Butter and flour an 8 1/2- by-4 1/2-inch loaf pan. Put the butter in the bowl of an electric mixer. Add the sugar and beat to blend. One at a time, add the eggs, beating continuously. Slowly add the flour and baking powder, beating until it is creamy and smooth. Set the butter aside. In a small bowl, combine the tangerines with 1 tablespoon flour and toss to coat. Add the tangerines to the batter, gently stirring to combine evenly.

2. Scrape the batter into the pan. Bake for 5 minutes, then reduce the temperature to 350°F and bake for 45 to 55 minutes more, until a toothpick inserted into the center comes out clean. Remove the cake from the oven, sprinkle on the Cointreau, transfer to a wire rack, and let cool at least 15 minutes. When cooled, slide a thin knife around the loaf to detach and remove from the pan. Serve at room temperature.

SOPHIE'S SWEET AND
SAVORY LOAVES

Winter

Roquefort, Bacon, and Walnut Loaf

Serves 6 to 8

1 tablespoon sunflower oil

2 ounces sliced bacon, cut into thin strips

1/2 cup walnuts, crushed

Fine sea salt

Freshly ground black pepper

3 large eggs

1 cup plus 2 tablespoons all-purpose flour, sifted

1 3/4 teaspoons baking powder

3 tablespoons peanut oil

3 tablespoons walnut oil

1/2 cup milk, hot

1 1/4 cups grated Gruyère cheese

3/4 cup crumbled Roquefort or blue cheese

1. Preheat the oven to 350°F. In a skillet, heat the sunflower oil over medium-high heat. Add the bacon and cook for 2 minutes, or until the pieces begin to separate, then reduce the heat to low. Stir in the nuts, a pinch of salt, and 2 pinches of pepper and cook for 5 minutes more. Set aside.

2. In the bowl of an electric mixer, beat the eggs, flour, and baking powder until smooth. Gradually add the peanut and walnut oils, beating constantly to blend. Gradually add the milk, beating constantly to blend. Stir in the Gruyère. Set the batter aside. Crumble the Roquefort over the bacon, stir to combine, then add to the batter.

3. Scrape the batter into an ungreased 8 1/2-by-4 1/2-inch loaf pan. Bake in the center of the oven for 45 to 55 minutes, until a toothpick inserted into the center comes out clean. Transfer the pan to a wire rack and let cool for at least 15 minutes, then slide a thin knife around the loaf and remove from the pan. Serve warm or at room temperature.

Foie Gras and Smoked Duck Breast Loaf

Serves 6 to 8

3 large eggs

1 cup plus 2 tablespoons all-purpose flour, sifted

1 3/4 teaspoons baking powder

3 tablespoons sunflower oil

1/2 cup milk, hot

Fine sea salt

Freshly ground black pepper

1 1/4 cups grated Gruyère cheese

4 ounces foie gras, cut into 1/2-inch cubes

6 ounces smoked duck breast, cut into thin strips

1/4 cup sliced almonds, toasted in a nonstick skillet until light brown

1. Preheat the oven to 350°F. In the bowl of an electric mixer, beat the eggs, flour, and baking powder until smooth. Gradually add the oil, beating constantly to blend. Gradually add the milk, beating constantly to blend. Add a pinch of salt, 2 pinches of pepper, and the cheese and stir to combine. Stir in the foie gras, duck breast, and half of the almonds.

2. Scrape the batter into an ungreased 8 1/2-by-4 1/2-inch loaf pan and sprinkle on the remaining almonds. Bake in the center of the oven for 45 to 55 minutes, until a toothpick inserted into the center comes out clean. Transfer the pan to a wire rack and let cool for at least 15 minutes, then slide a thin knife around the loaf and remove from the pan. Serve warm or at room temperature.

SOPHIE'S SWEET AND
SAVORY LOAVES

Smoked Salmon Loaf

Serves 6 to 8

3 large eggs

1 cup plus 2 tablespoons all-purpose flour, sifted

1 3/4 teaspoons baking powder

Fine sea salt

Freshly ground black pepper

1/3 cup plus 2 tablespoons sunflower oil

1/2 cup milk, hot

1 1/4 cups grated Gruyère cheese

7 ounces smoked salmon, cut into thin strips

10 chives, snipped into small pieces

1. Preheat the oven to 350°F. In the bowl of an electric mixer, beat the eggs, flour, baking powder, a pinch of salt, and 2 pinches of pepper until smooth. Gradually add the oil, beating constantly until blended. Gradually add the milk, beating constantly until well blended and no lumps remain. Add the cheese, stir to combine, then stir in the salmon and chives.

2. Scrape the batter into an ungreased 8 1/2-by-4 1/2-inch loaf pan. Bake in the center of the oven for 45 to 55 minutes, until a toothpick inserted into the center comes out clean. Transfer the pan to a wire rack and let cool for at least 15 minutes, then slide a thin knife around the loaf to detach and remove from the pan. Serve warm or at room temperature.

Candied Melon, Prune, and Dried Apricot Cake

Serves 6 to 8

3 ounces candied melon or citron, cut into small pieces

3 ounces pitted prunes, cut into small pieces

3 ounces dried apricots, cut into small pieces

2 tablespoons apricot liqueur

1 cup confectioners' sugar

1 stick plus 1 tablespoon (9 tablespoons) salted butter, softened

3 eggs

1 cup plus 3 tablespoons all-purpose flour, sifted

3/4 teaspoon baking powder

1. Preheat the oven to 450°F. Combine the fruits and apricot liqueur in a small bowl. Set aside. In the bowl of an electric mixer, cream the sugar and butter until light and smooth. One at a time, add the eggs and beat to combine. Add all but 1 tablespoon of the flour, and baking powder, and beat to blend. Set the batter aside. Drain the fruit, reserving the liquid. Toss the fruits with the remaining 1 tablespoon flour, turning to coat the pieces lightly, then gently fold into the batter.

2. Scrape the batter into an ungreased 8 1/2-by-4 1/2-inch loaf pan. Bake in the center of the oven for 5 minutes, reduce the heat to 350°F, and continue baking for 45 to 55 minutes, until a toothpick inserted into the center comes out clean. Transfer the pan to a wire rack and let cool at least 15 minutes, then slide a thin knife around the loaf and remove from the pan. Serve at room temperature.

Coffee-Chocolate-Whiskey Cake

Serves 6 to 8

3 large eggs

1 cup sugar

1 stick plus 1 tablespoon (9 tablespoons) salted butter, softened

1 1/2 cups all-purpose flour, sifted

3/4 teaspoon baking powder

1 1/4 cup milk

2 tablespoons unsweetened cocoa powder

4 tablespoons Scotch whiskey

1 tablespoon very strong coffee

1. Preheat the oven to 350°F. Butter and flour an 8 1/2-by-4 1/2-inch loaf pan. In the bowl of an electric mixer, beat the eggs and sugar until smooth. Add the butter and beat until smooth. Slowly add the flour and baking powder, beating until blended. Set the batter aside.

2. In a small saucepan, heat the milk over medium heat until small bubbles form around the edge of the pan. Add the cocoa and whisk until smooth. Add the whiskey and coffee and stir to blend. Pour the liquid into the batter and stir to incorporate.

3. Scrape the batter into the pan. Bake in the center of the oven for 55 to 65 minutes, until a toothpick inserted into the center comes out clean. Transfer the pan to a wire rack and let cool for at least 15 minutes, then slide a thin knife around the loaf and remove from the pan. Serve at room temperature.

125

SOPHIE'S SWEET AND SAVORY LOAVES

Fruitcake

Serves 6 to 8

2/3 cup currants

1 tea bag, preferably black Chinese or Indian tea

4 tablespoons dark or light rum

2 ounces candied cherries, cut into small pieces

2 ounces candied oranges, cut into small pieces

2 ounces candied citron, cut into small pieces

3/4 ounce candied angelica, cut into small pieces

1 cup plus 3 tablespoons all-purpose flour, sifted

1 stick plus 2 tablespoons (10 tablespoons) salted butter

1 cup confectioners' sugar

3 large eggs

3/4 teaspoon baking powder

1. Preheat the oven to 450°F. In a small bowl, combine the currants with the tea bag and rum. Pour enough warm water to cover and set aside. In a separate bowl, toss the candied fruits and angelica with 1 tablespoon of the flour to coat lightly.

2. In the bowl of an electric mixer, cream the butter and sugar until light and fluffy. One at a time, add the eggs then add the remaining flour except for 1 tablespoon and the baking powder and beat until smooth. Set the batter aside.

3. Drain the currants, reserving the liquid, and blot dry on paper towels. Toss with the remaining flour, then add them to the batter along with the other fruit.

4. Scrape the batter into an ungreased 8 1/2-by-4 1/2-inch loaf pan. Bake in the center of the oven for 5 minutes, then reduce the heat to 350°F and continue baking for 40 to 50 minutes more, until a toothpick inserted into the center comes out clean. Sprinkle on the reserved soaking liquid. Transfer the pan to a wire rack and let cool for at least 15 minutes, then slide a thin knife around the loaf and remove from the pan. Serve warm or at room temperature.

Variation: For Caramel-Almond-Raisin Cake,
caramelize sugar by cooking 1/2 cup granulated sugar and 6 tablespoons
water in a small saucepan. Just when the sugar is golden brown, quickly pour
it into the batter and mix well. Add 2/3 cup raisins that have been plumped
in warm water then drained and 3/4 cup toasted whole almonds.

Anise Cake

Serves 6 to 8

1 tablespoon butter for the pan

4 large eggs, separated

3/4 cup plus 2 tablespoons sugar

Grated zest of 1/2 lemon

2/3 cup plus 1 1/2 tablespoons all-purpose flour, sifted

Fine sea salt

1 tablespoon ground anise seed

1. Preheat the oven to 350°F. Butter and flour an 8 1/2-by-4 1/2-inch loaf pan. In the bowl of an electric mixer, combine the egg yolks with half of the sugar and beat until pale yellow and fluffy. Gradually add 3 1/2 tablespoons water and beat to blend. Add the lemon zest, flour, a pinch of salt, and the anise and beat to incorporate. Set the batter aside.
2. In the bowl of an electric mixer, combine the egg whites with the remaining sugar and beat until they hold soft peaks. Using a rubber spatula, gently fold them into the batter, working carefully to maintain as much volume as possible.
3. Scrape the batter into the pan. Bake in the center of the oven for 40 to 50 minutes, until a toothpick inserted into the center comes out clean. Transfer the pan to a wire rack and let cool for at least 15 minutes, then slide a thin knife around the loaf and remove from the pan. Serve at room temperature.

Candied Chestnut Cake

Serves 6 to 8

1/2 pound candied chestnuts, crumbled

2 tablespoons Cointreau or other orange-flavored liqueur

2 large eggs

3/4 cups plus 1 tablespoon sugar

1 (6-ounce) container plain yogurt (3/4 cup)

1 cup plus 2 tablespoons all-purpose flour, sifted

3/4 teaspoon baking powder

1/3 cup plus 2 tablespoons sunflower oil

1 tablespoon sweetened chestnut puree

1. Preheat the oven to 350°F. Butter and flour an 8 1/2-by-4 1/2-inch loaf pan. In a small bowl, combine the chestnuts and Cointreau and stir to combine. Set aside for 15 minutes.
2. In the bowl of an electric mixer, beat the eggs and sugar together until light and fluffy. Add the yogurt, all but 1 tablespoon of the flour, and the baking powder, beating constantly to blend, making sure no lumps remain. Gradually add the oil, then the chestnut puree, and beat to incorporate. Set aside.
3. Drain the chestnuts, reserving the liquid. Toss with the remaining 1 tablespoon flour, then add them to the batter and gently mix to combine.
4. Scrape the batter into the pan. Bake in the center of the oven for 40 to 50 minutes, until a toothpick inserted into the center comes out clean. Transfer the pan to a wire rack. Sprinkle on the reserved liquid and let cool for at least 15 minutes, then slide a thin knife around the loaf and remove from the pan. Serve at room temperature.

129

Auvergne-Style Loaf

Serves 6 to 8

1/3 cup plus 2 tablespoons sunflower oil

4 ounces white mushrooms, wiped, trimmed, and minced

Fine sea salt

4 ounces thin-sliced boiled ham, chopped

4 ounces tomme d'Auvergne cheese or Emmental cheese, cut into small cubes

3 large eggs

1 cup plus 2 tablespoons all-purpose flour, sifted

1 3/4 teaspoons baking powder

1/2 cup milk, hot

Freshly ground pepper

1 1/4 cups grated Gruyère cheese

1.   Preheat the oven to 350°F. In a skillet over high heat, heat 1 tablespoon of the oil, then add the mushrooms and sauté, stirring frequently, until all the liquid has evaporated. Remove from the heat, add a pinch of salt, the ham, and the tomme and stir to combine. Set aside.

2.   In the bowl of an electric mixer, combine the eggs, flour, and baking powder and beat until smooth. Gradually add the remaining oil, beating constantly until blended, then add the milk and beat until smooth. Add a pinch of pepper and the Gruyère, mix, then add the mushroom-ham mixture and stir to incorporate.

3.   Scrape the batter into an ungreased 8 1/2-by-4 1/2-inch loaf pan. Bake in the center of the oven for 45 to 55 minutes, until a toothpick inserted into the center comes out clean. Transfer the pan to a wire rack and let cool for at least 15 minutes, then slide a thin knife around the loaf and remove from the pan. Serve warm or at room temperature.

Smoked Sausage and Livarot Cheese Loaf

Serves 6 to 8

Leaves from 2 small sprigs fresh rosemary, finely chopped

4 ounces livarot, Pont l'Évêque, or Muenster cheese, cut into 1/2-inch cubes

1/3 cup plus 3 tablespoons sunflower oil

5 1/2 ounces precooked smoked pork sausage, such as knockwurst

1 clove garlic, minced

10 juniper berries, crushed

Fine sea salt

Freshly ground black pepper

3 large eggs

1 cup plus 2 tablespoons all-purpose flour, sifted

1 3/4 teaspoons baking powder

1/2 cup milk, hot

1 1/4 cups grated Gruyère cheese

1. Preheat the oven to 350°F. Sprinkle the rosemary over the livarot cheese and refrigerate. In a skillet, heat 1 tablespoon oil over medium heat. Add the sausage, garlic, and juniper berries. Cover and cook for 5 minutes, stirring occasionally, until warm. Season with a pinch of salt and 2 pinches of pepper. Set aside.

2. In the bowl of an electric mixer, combine the eggs, flour, and baking powder and beat until smooth. Gradually add the remaining oil, beating constantly until combined, then add the milk, beating constantly until smooth. Add the Gruyère and stir to combine. Cut the sausage into thin slices and stir into the batter.

3. Scrape the batter into an ungreased 8 1/2-by-4 1/2-inch loaf pan. Dot the top with the livarot cheese. Bake in the center of the oven for 45 to 55 minutes, until a toothpick inserted into the center comes out clean. Transfer the pan to a wire rack and let cool for at least 15 minutes, then slide a thin knife around the loaf and remove from the pan. Serve warm or at room temperature.

Flammenküchen: Alsatian Onion and Bacon Loaf

Serves 6 to 8

1 tablespoon salted butter

1/3 cup plus 3 tablespoons sunflower oil

1 medium onion, minced

7 ounces sliced smoked bacon, cut into 1/2-inch dice, or slab bacon, rind removed, cut into small dice

Fine sea salt

Freshly ground black pepper

1 tablespoon heavy cream

3 large eggs

1 cup plus 2 tablespoons all-purpose flour, sifted

1 3/4 teaspoons baking powder

1/2 cup milk, hot

1 1/4 cups grated Gruyère cheese

1. Preheat the oven to 350°F. In a skillet, combine the butter and 1 tablespoon oil and heat over medium-high heat. Add the onion and sauté, stirring frequently, until the onion begins to color. Add the bacon and continue cooking until the onions are golden brown. Season with a pinch each of salt and pepper. Remove from the heat, add the cream, and stir to combine. Set aside.

2. In the bowl of an electric mixer, combine the eggs, flour, and baking powder and beat until smooth. Gradually add the remaining oil, stirring constantly until blended, then add the milk, stirring constantly until smooth. Add the cheese, stir with a wooden spoon to combine, then add the onion-bacon mixture and stir until incorporated.

3. Scrape the batter into an ungreased 8 1/2-by-4 1/2-inch loaf pan. Bake in the center of the oven for 45 to 55 minutes, until a toothpick inserted into the center comes out clean. Transfer the pan to a wire rack and let cool for at least 15 minutes, then slide a thin knife around the loaf and remove from the pan. Serve warm or at room temperature.

SOPHIE'S SWEET AND SAVORY LOAVES

Candied Fruit Jellies Cake

Serves 6 to 8

1 stick plus 1 tablespoon (9 tablespoons) salted butter

1 cup confectioners' sugar

3 large eggs

1 cup plus 1 1/2 tablespoons all-purpose flour, sifted

3/4 teaspoon baking powder

7 ounces mixed jellied fruit candies, such as orange, apricot,
apple, or strawberry, finely chopped

1/2 cup whole unblanched shelled almonds, finely chopped

2 tablespoons Grand Marnier, or other liqueur of your choice

1.   Preheat the oven to 350°F. In the bowl of an electric mixer, cream the butter and sugar together until light and fluffy. One at a time, add the eggs, beating to incorporate, then add the flour and baking powder and beat to blend. Add the candies and almonds and stir to combine.

2.   Scrape the batter into an ungreased 8 1/2-by-4 1/2-inch loaf pan. Bake in the center of the oven for 45 to 55 minutes, until a toothpick inserted into the center comes out clean. Remove the cake from the oven, sprinkle on the liqueur, and immediately invert the pan; place the cake, right side up, on a wire rack and let cool. Serve at room temperature.

Almond Cake

Serves 6 to 8

2 large eggs

3/4 cup plus 1 tablespoon sugar

1 (6-ounce) container plain yogurt (3/4 cup)

1 cup plus 2 tablespoons all-purpose flour, sifted

3/4 teaspoon baking powder

1/3 cup plus 2 tablespoons sunflower oil

3/4 cup slivered almonds, ground to a coarse powder

1/3 cup sliced almonds

1. Preheat the oven to 350°F. Butter and flour an 8 1/2-by-4 1/2-inch loaf pan. In the bowl of an electric mixer, beat together the eggs and sugar. Add the yogurt and beat until blended. Combine the flour and baking powder and add to the mixture, beating well to blend. Gradually add the oil, beating to blend. The batter should be smooth and without lumps. Add the ground almonds and half of the sliced almonds and stir to combine.

2. Scrape the batter into the pan and sprinkle on the remaining almonds. Bake in the center of the oven for 45 to 55 minutes, until a toothpick inserted into the center comes out clean. Transfer the pan to a wire rack and let cool for at least 15 minutes, then slide a thin knife around the loaf and remove from the pan. Serve warm or at room temperature.

SOPHIE'S SWEET AND SAVORY LOAVES

Cinnamon-Coconut Cake

Serves 6 to 8

2 large eggs

3/4 cup plus 1 tablespoon sugar

1 (6-ounce) container plain yogurt (3/4 cup)

1 cup plus 2 tablespoons all-purpose flour, sifted

3/4 teaspoon baking powder

1 teaspoon ground cinnamon

2 tablespoons sweetened chestnut puree

1/3 cup plus 2 tablespoons sunflower oil

1 cup shredded unsweetened coconut

1. Preheat the oven to 350°F. Butter and flour an 8 1/2-by-4 1/2-inch loaf pan. In the bowl of an electric mixer, combine the eggs and sugar and beat until smooth. Add the yogurt, beating until blended. In a small bowl, combine the flour, baking powder, and cinnamon. Add them to the egg mixture, along with the chestnut puree, and beat to blend. Gradually add the oil and beat until well blended. The batter should be smooth and without any lumps. Add the coconut and stir to combine.

2. Scrape the batter into the pan. Bake in the center of the oven for 45 to 55 minutes, until a toothpick inserted into the center comes out clean. Transfer the pan to a wire rack and let cool for at least 15 minutes, then slide a thin knife around the loaf and remove from the pan. Serve at room temperature.

Praline Cake

Serves 6 to 8

2 large eggs

3/4 cup plus 1 tablespoon sugar

1 (6-ounce) container plain yogurt (3/4 cup)

1 cup plus 2 tablespoons all-purpose flour, sifted

3/4 teaspoon baking powder

1/3 cup plus 2 tablespoons sunflower oil

4 ounces almond brittle, coarsely chopped

1. Preheat the oven to 350°F. Butter and flour an 8 1/2-by-4 1/2-inch loaf pan. In the bowl of an electric mixer, combine the eggs and sugar and beat until smooth. Add the yogurt and beat until smooth. In a small bowl, combine the flour and baking powder, add to the egg mixture, and beat to blend. Gradually add the oil, beating constantly until blended. The batter should be smooth and without any lumps. Add the almond brittle and gently stir to combine.

2. Scrape the batter into the pan. Bake in the center of the oven for 45 to 55 minutes, until a toothpick inserted into the center comes out clean. Transfer the pan to a wire rack and let cool for at least 15 minutes, then slide a thin knife around the loaf and remove from the pan. Serve at room temperature.

Variations: For Praline-Chocolate Cake, add 4 ounces melted
dark chocolate with a high cocoa content to the batter, and reduce the
amount of almond brittle to 2 ounces. For Praline-Chocolate Chip Cake,
add 1/2 cup chocolate chips, dusted with flour, to the batter,
and reduce the amount of almond brittle to 2 ounces.

Savoyard Onion, Two-Cheese, and Bacon Loaf

Serves 6 to 8

1 tablespoon salted butter	4 ounces Reblochon cheese
1/3 cup plus 3 tablespoons sunflower oil	3 large eggs
1 medium onion, minced	1 cup plus 2 tablespoons all-purpose flour, sifted
1/4 pound slab bacon, rind removed, cut into 1-by-1/4-by-1/4-inch strips	1 3/4 teaspoons baking powder
Fine sea salt	1/2 cup milk, hot
Freshly ground black pepper	1 1/4 cups grated Gruyère cheese

1. Preheat the oven to 350°F. In a skillet, combine the butter and 1 tablespoon oil and heat over medium-high heat. Add the onion and sauté, stirring frequently, until the onion begins to color, about 4 minutes. Add the bacon and continue cooking, stirring frequently, until the onion is golden brown. Season with a pinch each of salt and pepper. Remove from the heat, add the Reblochon, and stir to combine. Set aside.

2. In the bowl of an electric mixer, combine the eggs, flour, and baking powder and beat until smooth. Gradually add the remaining oil, beating constantly until blended, then add the milk, beating constantly until blended. Add the Gruyère, stir to combine, then add the onion mixture to the batter and stir to combine.

3. Scrape the batter into an ungreased 8 1/2-by-4 1/2-inch loaf pan. Bake in the center of the oven for 45 to 55 minutes, until a toothpick inserted into the center comes out clean. Transfer the pan to a wire rack and let cool for at least 15 minutes, then slide a thin knife around the loaf and remove from the pan. Serve warm or at room temperature.

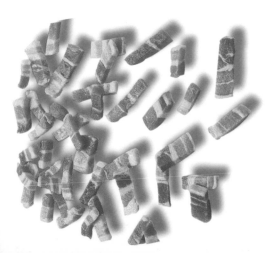

Sausage, Tomato, and Onion Loaf

Serves 6 to 8

2 tablespoons salted butter

1/3 cup plus 3 tablespoons sunflower oil

1 large, firm, ripe tomato, peeled, seeded, and diced large

1 large onion, minced

Fine sea salt

Freshly ground black pepper

1/2 teaspoon celery salt

3 large eggs

1 cup plus 2 tablespoons all-purpose flour, sifted

1 3/4 teaspoons baking powder

1/2 cup milk, hot

1 1/4 cups grated Gruyère cheese

6 ounces soppressata sausage, thinly sliced then cut into approximately 1/2-inch squares

1. Preheat the oven to 350°F. In a skillet, combine the butter and 1 tablespoon of the oil and heat over medium heat. Add the tomato and onion, stir to combine, then cook, stirring frequently, for 15 minutes. Add a pinch each of salt and pepper, the celery salt, stir to combine, then set aside to cool.

2. In the bowl of an electric mixer, combine the eggs, flour, and baking powder and beat until smooth. Gradually add the oil, beating constantly until blended, then add the milk, beating constantly until blended. Add the cheese and stir to combine. Add the sausage to the tomato and onion, stir to combine, then add to the batter, stirring to incorporate.

3. Scrape the batter into an ungreased 8 1/2-by-4 1/2-inch loaf pan. Bake in the center of the oven for 45 to 55 minutes, until a toothpick inserted into the center comes out clean. Transfer the pan to a wire rack and let cool for at least 15 minutes, then slide a thin knife around the loaf and remove from the pan. Serve warm or at room temperature.

Variation: For Sausage and Camembert Loaf, omit the tomato and onion *and add 4 ounces Camembert cheese cut into small cubes.*

Chorizo and Pont l'Évêque Cheese Loaf

Serves 6 to 8

3 large eggs

1 cup plus 2 tablespoons all-purpose flour, sifted

1 3/4 teaspoons baking powder

1/3 cup plus 2 tablespoons sunflower oil

3 tablespoons light lager beer

1/2 cup milk, hot

Fine sea salt

Freshly ground black pepper

1 1/4 cups grated Gruyère cheese

6 ounces chorizo, cut into 1/4-inch slices

4 ounces Pont l'Évêque or maroilles cheese, cut into 1/4-inch cubes

1/2 teaspoon ground cumin

1. Preheat the oven to 350°F. In the bowl of an electric mixer, combine the eggs, flour, and baking powder and beat until smooth. Gradually add the oil, then the beer, then the milk, beating each addition to blend. Add a pinch each of salt and pepper, the Gruyère, and the chorizo and stir to incorporate.

2. Scrape the batter into an ungreased 8 1/2-by-4 1/2-inch loaf pan. In a small bowl, mix the Pont l'Évêque with the cumin. Scatter the Pont l'Évêque over the top. Bake in the center of the oven for 45 to 55 minutes, until a toothpick inserted into the center comes out clean. Transfer the pan to a wire rack and let cool for at least 15 minutes, then slide a thin knife around the loaf and remove from the pan. Serve warm or at room temperature.

Bacon-Raclette Loaf

Serves 6 to 8

3 large eggs

1 cup plus 2 tablespoons all-purpose flour, sifted

1 3/4 teaspoons baking powder

Freshly ground black pepper

1/3 cup plus 2 tablespoons sunflower oil

1/2 cup milk, hot

1 1/4 cups grated Gruyère cheese

3 ounces raclette cheese, cut into small cubes

6 ounces Canadian bacon, cut into thin strips

1. Preheat the oven to 350°F. In the bowl of an electric mixer, combine the eggs, flour, baking powder, and a pinch of pepper and beat until smooth. Gradually add the oil, beating constantly until blended, then add the milk, beating constantly until blended. Add the Gruyère, stir to combine, then add the raclette and bacon and stir to combine.

2. Scrape the batter into an ungreased 8 1/2-by-4 1/2-inch loaf pan and bake in the center of the oven for 45 to 55 minutes, until a toothpick inserted into the center comes out clean. Transfer the pan to a wire rack and let cool for at least 15 minutes, then slide a thin knife around the loaf and remove from the pan. Serve warm or at room temperature.

151

SOPHIE'S SWEET AND SAVORY LOAVES

Lemon-Ginger-Whiskey Cake

Serves 6 to 8

6 ounces candied lemon peel, diced small

2 ounces candied ginger, diced small

2 tablespoons Scotch whiskey

1 cup confectioners' sugar

1 stick plus 1 tablespoon (9 tablespoons) salted butter, softened

3 large eggs

1 cup plus 3 tablespoons all-purpose flour, sifted

3/4 teaspoon baking powder

1. Preheat the oven to 450°F. In a small bowl, combine the lemon peel, ginger, and whiskey. Set aside. In the bowl of an electric mixer, cream the sugar and butter together until light and fluffy. One at a time, add the eggs, beating to incorporate, then add all but 1 tablespoon of the flour and the baking powder and beat until smooth. Set the batter aside. Strain the lemons and ginger, reserving the liquid. Toss with the remaining 1 tablespoon flour, turning to coat, then add to the batter and stir to combine.

2. Scrape the batter into an ungreased 8-inch heart-shaped baking pan, or an 8-inch round pan. Bake in the center of the oven for 5 minutes, then reduce the temperature to 350°F and continue baking for 40 to 50 minutes more, until a toothpick inserted into the center comes out clean. Remove the pan from the oven, pour on the reserved liquid, transfer to a wire rack, and let cool for at least 15 minutes. Slide a thin knife around the loaf and remove from the pan. Serve at room temperature.

Honey-Walnut Cake

Serves 6 to 8

1/2 cup sugar

7 tablespoons salted butter, softened

2 tablespoons honey

1 cup plus 3 tablespoons all-purpose flour, sifted

3/4 teaspoon baking powder

3 large eggs

3/4 cup walnuts, chopped

2 tablespoons Grand Marnier

1. Preheat the oven to 450°F. Butter and flour an 8 1/2-by-4 1/2-inch loaf pan. In the bowl of an electric mixer, cream the sugar and butter until smooth. Add the honey, flour, and baking powder, beating after each to combine. One at a time, add the eggs and beat to blend. Add the walnuts and stir to combine.

2. Scrape the batter into the pan. Bake in the center of the oven for 5 minutes, then reduce the temperature to 350°F, and bake for 40 to 50 minutes more, until a toothpick inserted into the center comes out clean. Remove the pan from the oven, sprinkle on the Grand Marnier, transfer to a wire rack, and let cool for at least 15 minutes. Then slide a thin knife around the cake and remove from the pan, return the cake, right side up, to the wire rack to cool. Serve at room temperature.

Variation: For Honey-Hazelnut Cake, omit the walnuts and add the same amount of chopped hazelnuts.

155

SOPHIE'S SWEET AND
SAVORY LOAVES

Sophie's Notes

Tips and Tricks for Creating the Best Loaves and Cakes

Instead of using a standard loaf pan, you can substitute a specialized decorative cake pan—perhaps a heart or a star, a bunny or a wreath—to make your cake or loaf more festive. The batters also lend themselves to cooking in a muffin tin, with slightly reduced cooking times.

When using a vanilla bean, scrape out the seeds for the recipe, but save the pods for making vanilla sugar: Use one vanilla bean, split lengthwise, for each cup of sugar. Combine the pods and the sugar in a jar, then seal securely and set aside for several weeks to allow the perfume and flavor of the vanilla to infuse the sugar. Use where regular sugar is called for in the sweet recipes here, as well as in other sweet recipes.

I always use whole milk when I bake, which makes the cakes richer, but you can always substitute partially skimmed 2% milk.

I prefer that the oven rack on which I place my pans be cold so that the loaf or cake won't dry too quickly and stick to the bottom of the pan. I keep the oven rack on which I'll be baking out, and put it back in the oven only when the cake is ready to bake.

Your microwave oven can help you save time when you're peeling tomatoes or peaches: Place them in the microwave oven and cook for 1 minute at low power. The skin will peel off easily when they come out.

With rare exceptions, noted in the recipes, you should always allow your cake or loaf to cool before removing it from the pan.

I use sunflower oil almost exclusively in my cakes and loaves; the only exception is in recipes using Provençal ingredients, such as the Ratatouille Loaf, in which I use olive oil.

Take all of your ingredients out of the refrigerator ahead of time; ideally you should work with ingredients at room temperature.

When you have the time, let your batter sit for up to 30 minutes before you bake it, so that the flavors have time to permeate the batter and make the cake or loaf even more delicious.

You will notice that in some recipes, often those with candied fruits, that I toss them with flour before adding them to the batter. This technique helps incorporate them into the batter and keeps them from sinking to the bottom of the pan.

In chocolate desserts, I use dark chocolate with a cocoa content of 70%. Chocolate with a lower cocoa content may not have a rich enough flavor; with a higher cocoa content the flavor becomes too bitter.

The savory loaves are very versatile; you can serve them as hors d'oeuvres, cut into narrow fingers, or cubes; as an appetizer; or, along with a mixed green salad as a light main course for lunch or supper. If there are any leftovers, you can cut them into small cubes and toss them in a salad, like croutons.

Many loaves can be prepared ahead and stored in the refrigerator, wrapped in plastic wrap, for several days. Bring them to room temperature before serving. The savory loaves can be gently heated in the microwave for a few seconds before serving.

Guide to Specialty Stores

For a wide variety of olive and nut oils, salts, peppers, olives, sugars, vanilla beans, and much more, contact the following companies for information or a catalogue:

BALDUCCI'S
424 Avenue of the Americas
New York, NY 10011
Tel: 800-822-1444 or
212-673-2600

DEAN & DELUCA
560 Broadway
New York, NY 10012
Tel: 800-221-7714 or
212-226-6800
www.deananddeluca.com

FAUCHON
442 Park Avenue
New York, NY 10022
Tel: 212-308-5919
www.fauchon.com

SALUMERIA ITALIANA
151 Richmond Street
Boston, MA 02109-1414
Tel: 800-400-5916 or
617-523-8743
Fax: 617-523-4946

SWEET CELEBRATIONS INC.
P.O. Box 39426
Edina, MN 55439-0426
Tel: 800-328-6722 or
952-943-1508
www.sweetc.com

For excellent crème fraîche and other dairy products:

VERMONT BUTTER AND
CHEESE COMPANY
P.O. Box 95
Websterville, VT 05678
Tel: 800-884-6287 or
802-479-9371
www.vtbutterandcheeseco.com

For a selection of goat cheese, fresh, aged, and herbed:

LITTLE RAINBOW CHÈVRE
15 Doe Hill Road
Hillsdale, NY12529
Tel: 518-325-4628
www.littlerainbow.com

For a broad range of domestic and imported cheeses, cut to order before shipping, as well as crème fraîche:

IDEAL CHEESE SHOP, LTD.
942 First Avenue
New York, NY 10022
Tel: 800-382-0109 or
212-688-7579
Fax: 212-223-1245
www.idealcheese.com

For domestic foie gras and fresh ducks:

D'ARTAGNAN
152 East 46th Street
New York, NY 10017
Tel: 800-DARTAGN or
212-687-0300

For smoked eastern and western salmon:

DUCKTRAP RIVER FISH FARM
57 Little River Drive
Belfast, ME 04915
Tel: 800-828-3825 or
207-763-3960
Fax: 207-338-6288
www.ducktrap.com

For succulent Maine sea scallops, excellent seasonal fish, and exclusive lines of custom-smoked salmon:

BROWNE TRADING COMPANY:
260 Commercial Street
Merrill's Wharf
Portland, ME 04101
Tel: 800-944-7848 or
207-766-2404
Fax: 207-766-2404
www.browne-trading.com

For seasonal French produce, such as wild mushrooms and more:

MARCHÉ AUX DÉLICES
P.O. Box 1164
New York, NY 10028
Tel: 888-547-5471
Fax: 413-604-2789
www.auxdelices.com